Natural Resources of British Columbia and the Yukon

An Introduction

Natural Resources of British Columbia and the Yukon

Mary L. Barker

Douglas, David & Charles:
Vancouver

David & Charles:
Newton Abbot

Copyright© Mary L. Barker, 1977

Douglas, David & Charles Ltd.,
1875 Welch Street, North Vancouver, B.C.,
Published in Great Britain by
David & Charles (Holdings) Limited,
Newton Abbot, Devon

Canadian Cataloguing in Publication Data
    Barker, Mary L., 1945-
        Natural resources of British Columbia and
    the Yukon

        Includes bibliography and index.
        ISBN 0-88914-049-9

        1. Natural resources — British Columbia.
        2. Natural resources — Yukon Territory.
        I. Title.
        HC117.B8B37   333.7'09711   C77-002036-4
                                                77-2036
Library of Congress Catalog Card Number 76-49333

Jacket and book design by Nancy Legue
Typesetting by Domino-Link Word and Data Processing
Printed in Canada by Hemlock Printers Ltd., Burnaby
Bound by Trade Bindery Specialties Ltd., Vancouver

Acknowledgements

In the fall semester of 1975, Simon Fraser University offered an evening course entitled "The Natural Resources of British Columbia and the Yukon." It was given by the author and Dr. G.H. Eisbacher (Geological Survey of Canada). The enthusiastic response of our students suggested the need for an introduction to this topic in book form. No publication since Roderick Haig-Brown's *The Living Land* has attempted an overview of natural resources in British Columbia or the Yukon Territory.

Much has happened since 1961, but most of the information is available only in specialized government reports. These I have used freely in compiling the material for this book. For the sake of simplicity, I have avoided footnotes and references within the text. However, it is impossible to overestimate the value of information contained within the publications of Statistics Canada, provincial and federal resource agencies, and trade journals. The most important sources are listed in the back of the book.

I am particularly indebted to Dr. G.H. Eisbacher, who guided me through the voluminous literature relating to the mineral and energy resources of western Canada. Geri critically read large portions of the manuscript and contributed illustrations to the section on mineral and energy resources.

Ray Squirrel and Margaret Wheat, cartographers in the Department of Geography, Simon Fraser University, patiently drafted many of the maps, diagrams and graphs. My thanks to them and the Department of Geography for their support.

Dedicated to the memory of **Roderick Haig-Brown**,
who taught a generation to understand
this living land.

Contents

List of Tables

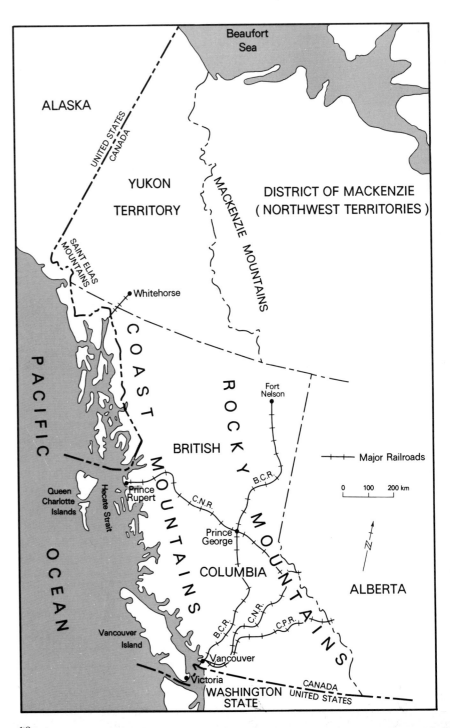

1 Introduction

British Columbia and the Yukon Territory are areas of strong physical contrasts. The landscape of the Canadian Cordillera is extremely varied, and its scale is difficult to grasp. Rugged offshore islands, deep fjords, and narrow coastal plains give way to high, glaciated coast mountains which stretch from the southern border of British Columbia to the Yukon-Alaska boundary. Toward the east, the rolling plateaus of the Interior are bordered by the Rocky Mountains, which offer the most spectacular scenery in Canada. The contrasts are heightened by a zoning of natural vegetation. The windward slopes capture the moist maritime air moving eastward from the Pacific Ocean, and the leeside of the mountains is dry. Farther north, an endless expanse of spruce forest and tundra dominates the landscape.

The variety of natural environments offered a wide choice of natural resources to European settlers who moved into the region during the nineteenth century. Western Canada's short history is one of spectacular surges of development based upon natural resources. The first explorers sought fur-bearing animals, but transportation posed a major problem. It took more than a year to transport supplies and furs between eastern Canada and isolated northern posts. The importance of the inland fur trade declined with the gold rushes to the Fraser River and the Cariboo country between 1858 and 1862. These discoveries brought the first large wave of settlers and spurred some clearance of agricultural land. Fisheries, based upon salmon to be canned for export, developed rapidly before the turn of the century, and canneries were established at most of the river mouths along the coast. Logging and sawmilling began to thrive with the first transcontinental railroad and the completion of the Panama Canal. Railways also provided an incentive for the exploitation of the mineral wealth of the Kootenays.

In the far north, the Klondike gold rush of 1898 brought the first large wave of white people to the Yukon. Soon after the turn of the century, the population of the territory dwindled to a few thousand, many of whom depended on trapping as they had before the rush.

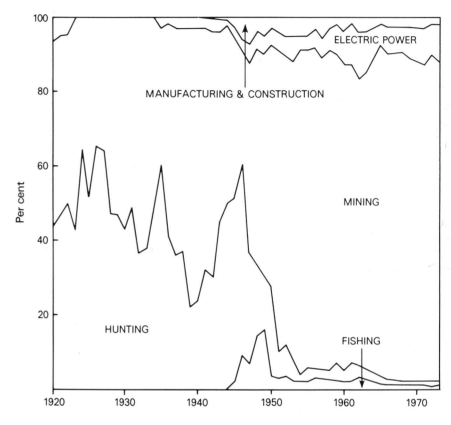

Resource developments in B.C. continued until the country was hit by the Depression. Forestry and mining, the mainstays of the B.C. economy, suffered severe losses, but eventually recovered. With World War II, the 2,500 kilometres of the Alaska Highway were pushed through the virgin north from Dawson Creek to Fairbanks, Alaska. However, the full effect of this military supply line was not felt until the 1950s and 60s, when mineral exploration expanded into areas accessible from the new road. The small Yukon economy, which had been based almost entirely on trapping, grew rapidly as new mines were brought into production (Figure 1).

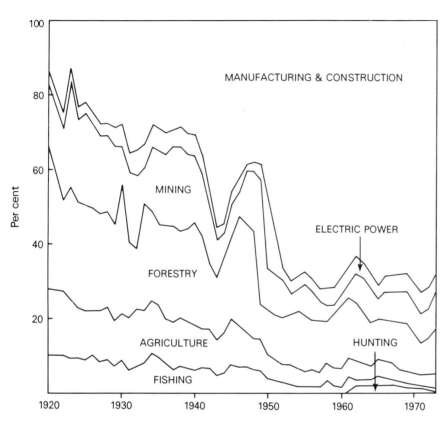

2 Net value of production in British Columbia, 1920-1973. The graph shows the relative contributions of hunting and trapping, fishing, agriculture, forestry, mining, electric power, manufacturing and construction to the economy. (Source: *Canada Year Book,* annual)

Changes in world markets, production technologies, and transportation have created booms and slumps, and their impact upon the geographical and political evolution of British Columbia and the Yukon cannot be underestimated.

The manufacturing industry of British Columbia, which underwent a major expansion only after 1945, is also based upon the extraction of natural resources. It is now dominated by the production of lumber, pulp and paper from timber, the refining of petroleum, and the processing of metal ores and fish. Other sectors of the economy, including hydro-electric power, construction, transportation, and trade, are linked closely to resource processing. The small manufacturing and construction industries of the Yukon Territory are supported largely by new mining developments.

The pattern of settlement shifted in accordance with whichever natural resource was preferred. Southwestern British Columbia is the core region of the province. There the forest industry grew up and still maintains the largest concentration of wood-processing plants. In spite of the fact that Victoria is the seat of the provincial legislature, Vancouver is the financial and commercial centre of British Columbia.

Elsewhere, settlements have been based upon the exploitation of particular resources. For example, Port Alice, Port Alberni, and Mackenzie depend upon the well-being of the forest industry. Trail, Atlin, Stewart, Dawson City, and Faro owe their origins to different periods of mining.

Shifts in the resource economy have been accompanied by changes in public attitudes toward natural resources. In the early days, resources were wastefully exploited because they were thought to be unlimited; the vision of endless forests, for example, encouraged environmentally unsound practices in the logging industry. Eventually, gold-rush towns were deserted because the ore was worked out. Wildlife species were threatened with extinction because of overhunting. Even the logging companies were forced to move farther afield once the accessible coastal sites had been cleared.

New roads encouraged logging and sawmilling in the Interior of British Columbia and, more recently, hydro-electric power projects and new mines. Although the total value of farm and fish products continues to climb, the relative importance of commercial fishing and agriculture in the B.C. economy is declining (Figure 2).

The economies of British Columbia and the Yukon have been and still are based on the extraction and processing of natural resources. Most of the province's wood products, minerals, natural gas, and fish are exported. The entire mineral production of the Yukon is exported for processing outside the territory, either elsewhere in Canada or abroad.

Some natural resources have definite limits and are *non-renewable*. For example, minerals and fossil fuels (i.e., coal and petroleum) have been created over such long geological time-spans that they cannot be replaced within any conceivable period of time. Once they are exhausted, exploration moves on in search of new ore-bodies, and sometimes it is necessary to look for substitutes.

Other natural resources, including forests, farmland, water, and wildlife are *renewable*, as long as they are not exploited more quickly than nature can replace them. Sustained yield management has been introduced to ensure that the rate of use does not exceed the rate at which the resource renews itself. This means placing limitations on fish catches and restrictions on the amount of timber logged. If the delicate balance between use and replacement can be maintained, a renewable resource can be maintained perpetually. If it is exploited too rapidly, it may become non-renewable: overhunting of some wildlife species has led to their extinction, and lakes can become so polluted that they are unattractive and unusable. Sustained yield management was first introduced to the West Coast fisheries during the 1930s, when salmon and halibut stocks were showing signs of depletion. Similarly, B.C. forests have been managed for sustained yield since 1953.

The most recent challenge has been an increasing pressure upon wilderness and recreational resources. The history of park creation in British Columbia and the Yukon clearly reflects the changing value of recreational resources. For a long period of time, parks had to be justified in terms of their economic return. A more enlightened approach is prevalent now. The balance between the economic needs of today and wise planning for the future must be sought in any policy of conservation. Mistakes made today cannot be undone tomorrow.

2 Minerals, Energy, and Water

In a modern society, it is taken for granted that homes are well heated, that they are equipped with electricity, that transportation between towns is rapid, and that food, water, and health services are available at all times. Such expectations can only be fulfilled if energy is continuously converted into electricity by burning fuels or taming rivers, if enough copper ore is found for transmission lines and generators, and if other metals are available to manufacture sophisticated steels, electronic gadgets, and cars. Our very existence clearly depends on the limited reserves of certain raw materials that are stored within the outer parts of the earth's crust as oil fields, coal seams, and metal ore deposits.

Some nations which are smaller and older than Canada have a mining history that may go back two or even three thousand years; they have already exploited their most accessible energy and mineral resources and must now resort to less accessible, leaner, and therefore more expensive resources. Other nations, lacking essential non-renewable resources altogether, must try to obtain them in exchange for skilfully manufactured goods.

The Cordilleran region of British Columbia and the Yukon Territory is relatively rich in fossil fuels and minerals. Within this mountainous area their distribution is uneven, and many of the most valuable deposits are confined to remote parts of the country. A piece of copper ore may travel thousands of kilometres before it reaches a smelter, and may make another trip halfway around the world before it finally becomes part of some electric equipment.

Fortunately for the exploration geologist, the distribution of energy and metal deposits, though uneven, is not entirely random. It follows a pattern related to the ancient geological history of the Cordillera, a history that goes back as far as one billion years. During this huge span of time, impossible to express in terms of human epochs, metal-bearing solutions ascended through the earth's crust, plant matter changed to coal, and tiny organisms decayed to form oil and gas. The distinct pattern which the geologist notes when mapping different rock formations enables him to distinguish areas with more or less promise of a certain metal or fuel resource. Areas which look good after the first reconnaissance are then carefully scanned by teams of prospectors. In its more refined stages, exploration is also aided by the chemical peculiarities of soils and streams near ore deposits (geochemical prospecting); by electric, magnetic, or mass properties of ore metals (geophysical prospecting); and by the elastic behaviour of sedimentary strata during the passage of seismic waves (seismic prospecting).

For a basic understanding of metal and energy resources in British Columbia and the Yukon Territory, the region can be divided into five belts spanning a distance of more than 1,500 kilometres from the United States border to the Arctic Ocean (Figure 3).

1. The *Eastern Sedimentary Belt* is underlain by strata of limestone, shale, and sandstone. In the plains of northeastern B.C. and the northern Yukon Territory, these strata lie horizontally and deeply incised rivers have carved broad table-shaped plateaus from the layered rocks. In the Rockies, the same strata were folded and ruptured during uplift of the mountain ranges; there too, rivers and glaciers combined to sculpture magnificent castles, ramparts and crags from the contorted formations of limestone. This Eastern Belt hosts most of the known oil, gas and coal of the region.

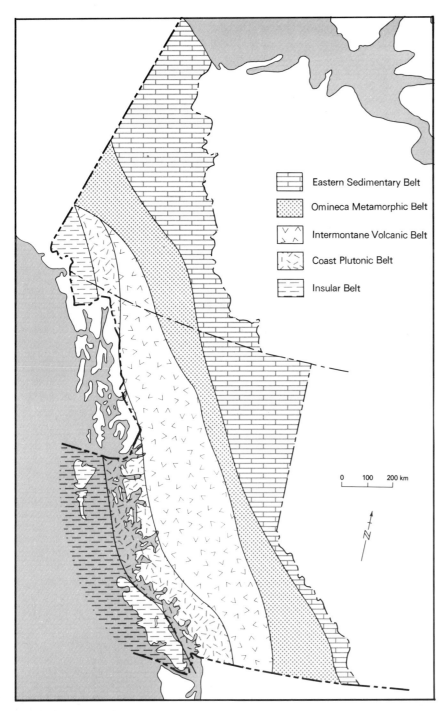

3 The five geological subdivisions of the Canadian Cordillera. Each of the belts is characterized by certain rock types and structures.

Eastern Sedimentary Belt

Omineca Metamorphic Belt

Intermontane Volcanic Belt

Coast Plutonic Belt

Insular Belt

0   100   200 km

2. The *Omineca Metamorphic Belt* is separated from the Eastern Belt by the Rocky Mountain Trench and other linear valleys. A large portion of the mountains in this belt consists of contorted crystalline schists and granitic intrusions. The schists are mostly ancient sedimentary rocks (e.g., limestones or sandstones) which, under high pressure and temperature, were converted into metamorphic rocks such as marble or mica schists. Later uplift and erosion made it possible to examine the mountain roots wherever outcroppings of rock protrude through the dense mantle of vegetation. The Omineca Belt has traditionally been an area of lead-zinc exploration.

3. The *Intermontane Volcanic Belt* is a large mosaic of ancient extrusive lava flows and deeply eroded intrusive complexes such as those of the famous copper porphyries. It is a zone of extensive plateaus and broad basins. Numerous lakes and silt banks bear witness to the fact that only about 10,000 years ago, large glaciers covered most of B.C. and the Yukon, and that the present dry climate of the Interior is of a more recent geological date.

4. The *Coast Plutonic Belt* rises in a chain of mountains, from Vancouver in the south to the Yukon in the north. The coarse intrusive rocks of quartz-diorite or granodiorite plutons are exposed in steep faces along the winding fjords of the coast and in precipitous pinnacles rising above the rain forest and the ice-covered uplands.

5. The *Insular Belt* consists of volcanic and intrusive rocks which form a ribbon of islands between Prince Rupert and Victoria. The largest members of this group are Vancouver Island and the Queen Charlotte Islands.

The subdivisions outlined above are also useful in understanding the course of rivers, the pattern of vegetation, and the history of settlement. From the outset, the search for precious metals and the milling of forest products followed the great valleys parallel to the trend of the Cordilleran mountain ranges. Later construction of railroads and highways over narrow passes has only slightly modified the principal access to the resources of western Canada.

Metals, oil, gas, and coal are non-renewable resources. Their exploitation follows a pattern of search, discovery, development, mining, and final exhaustion. However, the detailed history of each mining camp is more complicated than that. Changes in the price of metals, new means of transportation, new mining technology, or environmental safeguards have a profound effect on the life of any mine, but even the largest ore bodies eventually become exhausted. In British Columbia and the Yukon Territory, only thirty to forty mines can claim to have actually been worked for more than twenty years. Most of the 300 mines opened since the beginning of metal mining have closed for good; others may be revived temporarily for short periods of time. Thus, the regional pattern of mining is shifting constantly and is essentially unpredictable. However, the mining of new, large, low-grade deposits involves a considerable amount of planning.

Such ore bodies require great financial commitments, and the lifespan of the mine must be more than a few years to make it worthwhile. Therefore, the stage of development and appraisal prior to mining is increasingly important. In this sense, the large-scale copper mines of the Highland Valley in southern B.C. are hardly in the same category with the gold placers of the Klondike. Similarly, the large-scale, modern, hydro-electric power projects demand more planning of their total impact than their humble predecessors thirty or forty years ago.

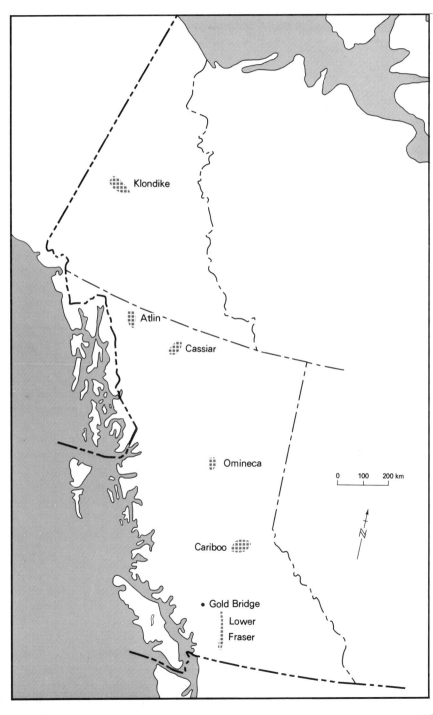

4 The distribution of the principal gold placer deposits in British Columbia and Yukon Territory.

Klondike

Atlin

Cassiar

Omineca

0   100   200 km

Cariboo

• Gold Bridge
  Lower
  Fraser

Gold

Gold and silver are considered *precious metals*. Their scarcity and beauty sets them apart from the more abundant *base metals* such as copper, lead or zinc. Much of the value of gold lies in the eyes of the beholder, and throughout history its magic has dominated the thinking of kings and conquistadors. Gold has been used in jewellery and as a stable form of payment. Even in this industrial age, only about five per cent of the gold production is refined for technological purposes.

In most mining districts of the world, gold was the first metal to attract the attention of the prospector, for it occurs freely as small particles or nuggets at the bottom of stream beds. From the earliest placer mines, prospecting soon expanded upstream and downstream. Sometimes even the mother lode of quartz veins, from which the river had originally eroded its gold, was found. The high value placed upon it in relation to its weight was the main reason for gold having been the target of the mining pioneers. Transportation in those days was generally even more primitive than the techniques of mining. However, simple as the pan, the long toms, and the rockers may have been, they paved the way for dredges and steam shovels which were used only when a creek was proven rich enough to justify the expense of bringing in heavier equipment.

Between 1850 and 1900, the history of British Columbia and the Yukon Territory was a series of gold rushes: waves of miners by the thousands. When the first signs of depletion and overworking appeared along the placer creeks of California, many miners eagerly joined in the rush northward into Canada. Within the next fifty years all the major gold placers of western Canada had been found: the lower Fraser River, 1858; the Cariboo, 1860; the Omineca Country, 1869; the Cassiar Mountains, 1873; the Klondike, 1896; Atlin, 1898 (Figure 4).

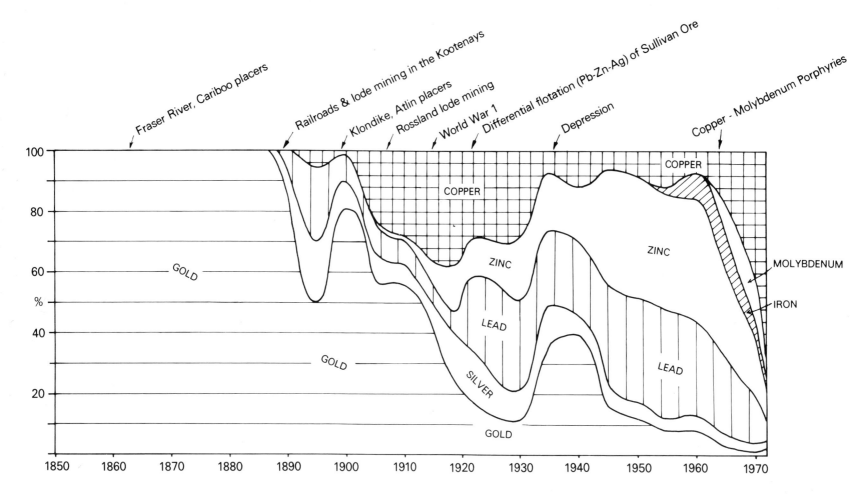

5 The relative contributions of gold, silver, lead, zinc, copper, iron and molybdenum to the value of the metal-mining industry of British Columbia and Yukon Territory, 1850-1970. The graph shows the predominance of gold in the beginning, lead-zinc in the 1950s and copper at present. (Source: B.C. Minister of Mines, Annual Reports)

Placer mining in western Canada followed the same history of eventual decline as elsewhere, and gold was soon overtaken by the growing need for base metals (Figure 5). At present, most of the gold produced in British Columbia and the Yukon Territory is a byproduct of base-metal deposits. Rising prices, however, have channeled interest back to the old placer camps of the Klondike, Atlin and Cariboo, and to the gold-bearing veins of the Omineca, Coast, and Insular Belts.

The lodes or *gold veins* are, as a rule, white stringers of quartz or carbonate rock that cut across country rock. The material found in veins was originally carried by solutions ascending through the outer parts of the earth's crust. The solutions moved through open fractures and faults, and dissolved chemical elements, including gold, were eventually precipitated as veins. Later uplift and erosion brought the veins within the reach of the prospector.

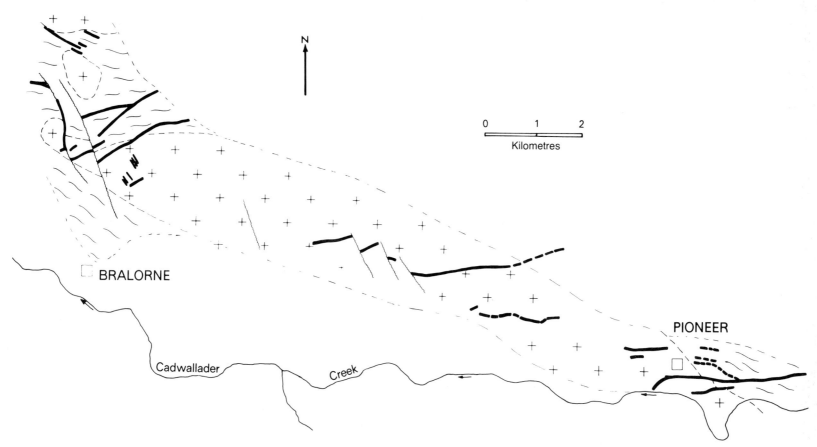

6 Map of the gold-bearing veins of the Bralorne-Pioneer mining camp in the Coast Plutonic Complex of southwestern British Columbia. (Simplified from Geological Survey of Canada Memoir 213)

Regionally, many of the gold-bearing veins are located within the Omineca and Coast Belts. Figure 6 is a sketch map showing the course of gold-bearing veins of the Bralorne-Pioneer camp, near Gold Bridge in southwestern B.C., which has been a focus of gold-mining and exploration for many years. The veins, which cut across ancient igneous and volcanic rocks, were mined mainly in underground workings.

When streams erode a channel across veins, the rushing water here and there picks up pieces of veins and gold. Given a very special set of conditions, the gold accumulates in pockets or placers within the river gravels. The *gold placers* of western Canada are found in such stream gravels, brought mainly from outcroppings of gold veins in the crystalline uplands. Within the gravels, the gold particles filter slowly downward through the sand, because of their heavier weight, and settle preferably in cracks and hollows of the bedrock channels. The resulting gold-bearing pay streaks were and still are sought out by the experienced prospector. Sometimes older and abandoned stream channels have yielded higher values of gold than the present stream beds. In the Klondike, the inexperienced miners—the Cheechakos—were the first ones to go after the White Channel Gravel high above the present stream beds and were rewarded with unexpected success. These high-level gravels are remnants of older river channels that filled the valleys before the present rivers carved their course into the Yukon Plateau.

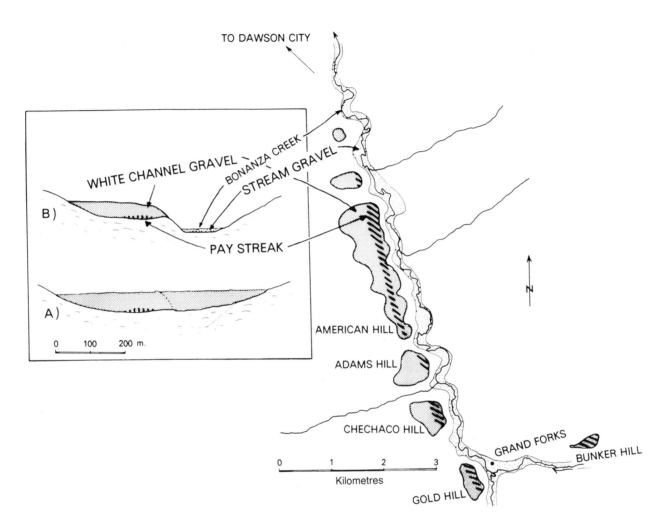

7 Map of the Bonanza Creek near Dawson City, Yukon Territory. The inset is a vertical cross-section through the valley at two stages of its evolution. A: an older, wider valley was filled up by the White Channel Gravels with concentration of gold along the main pay streak. B: during regional uplift, Bonanza Creek began to cut its bed into the White Channel Gravels and underlying bedrock, then reworked the gravel and some of its contained gold. (Simplified from Geological Survey of Canada Report 974, 1907)

In the case of the rich Klondike placers, the present creeks merely reworked the pay streak of the older White Channels (Figure 7). Placer mining opened the door to the Canadian West but, more than that, it was the beginning of a search for all the other metals that were to replace gold during the later part of the twentieth century (Figure 5). In British Columbia and the Yukon Territory, some of the finest historical resources relate to the gold-rush days. Increasing awareness of this unique period of Canadian history may help to preserve some of the buildings and machinery dating from those turbulent days.

Lead-Zinc-Silver

The mining of silver and lead goes back to the dawn of civilization. Silver gained a very special status in ancient Greek and Roman times because it was used as currency throughout the conquered regions of Europe, Asia and Africa. At present, however, most of the silver produced goes to the photographic and electrical industries. Lead is used extensively in storage batteries, and zinc is an anti-corrosive ingredient in steel and various alloys.

In ore deposits, lead, zinc, and silver are closely associated as sulphide minerals. The principal minerals are honey-brown sphalerite (ZnS) and grey-lustrous galena (PbS). Silver is contained in a variety of grey metallic sulphides, but also substitutes for lead in the crystal structure of galena.

The first notable mineral discovery in British Columbia preceded the famous gold rushes of the 1850s by quite a few years. In about 1825, the celebrated botanist David Douglas (after whom the Douglas fir is named) was studying the flora along the east shore of Kootenay Lake when he stumbled upon a large out-cropping of galena. Shortly afterward, trappers employed by the Hudson's Bay Company used the ore from this locality to replenish their supply of bullets. This showing was soon forgotten, but it was rediscovered by prospectors some thirty years later, when it eventually became the Bluebell Mine. In 1871, silver veins were discovered south of Fort Hope (now the town of Hope), but systematic lode-mining of silver, lead and zinc had to wait for the arrival of the railroads. The first regular production of silver-lead ore came from the Lanark Mine, a few kilometres east of Revelstoke along the new railroad, in 1887; the ore had to be shipped all the way to San Francisco to be smelted. The railroads precipitated not only the opening of several other lode mines in the Kootenays and the western Rockies but also numerous other discoveries of gold, silver, lead and zinc deposits, including the spectacular Sullivan mine.

8 Major areas of lead-zinc mineralization in British Columbia and Yukon Territory.

9 Vertical cross-section through the lead-zinc ore body of the Sullivan Mine near Kimberley, British Columbia. (Simplified from Canadian Institute of Mining and Metallurgy, Special Volume No. 8)

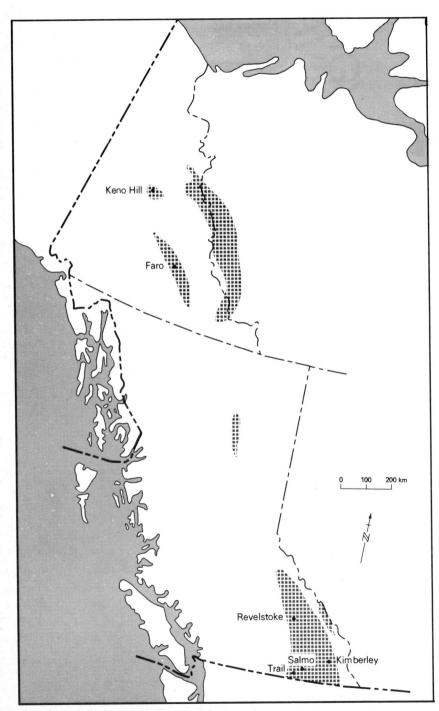

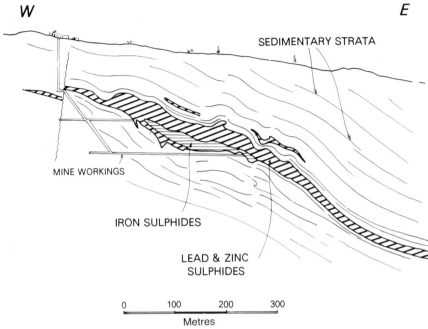

The bulk of the lead-zinc-silver resources of British Columbia and the Yukon Territory is lodged in rock formations of the Omineca and Eastern Belts (Figure 8). Two principal types of lead-zinc deposits have dominated the thinking of exploration geologists in the Cordilleran region: one group includes the stratiform ore bodies; the other group, the veins.

Stratiform ore deposits are parallel to the layering of the surrounding strata and therefore are also called concordant deposits. Their origin is thought to be related to the subsidence of wide sedimentary basins which existed in the Cordillera some 200 to 1,000 million years ago. Sand and clay filled the centre of these basins, and limestone platforms, similar to the present Bahama Banks, fringed the margins.

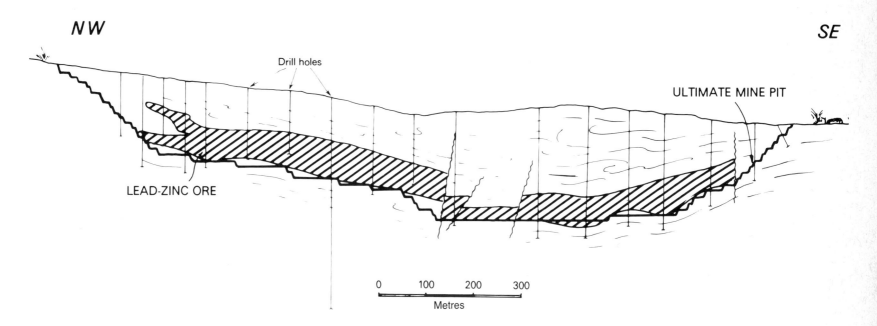

10 Schematic vertical cross-section through the Anvil lead-zinc mine near Faro, Yukon Territory. This also shows the location of drill-holes which determined the outline of the ore body and were used to design the ultimate outline of the mine pit. (Simplified from International Geological Congress Guidebook A24, 1972)

NW

SE

Drill holes

ULTIMATE MINE PIT

LEAD-ZINC ORE

0   100   200   300

Metres

Under special conditions, still poorly understood, metallic brines ascended slowly from the deeper parts near the centre of the basin and impregnated some of the sedimentary layers with metal-bearing sulphides. The mineralized zones are generally enriched in lead, zinc, silver, copper, gold, iron, tin, and other valuable elements, whose relative abundance varies from mine to mine. The ore-bearing strata may be relatively undeformed, such as those in the Sullivan Mine near Kimberley (Figure 9) or in the Faro ore body of the Anvil district in the Yukon (Figure 10). Cross-sections through these great ore bodies illustrate that, although the sedimentary host rock and its layered ores are tilted, they are only locally broken by faults. This cohesiveness of the ore body facilitates large-scale underground (e.g., Sullivan) or open-pit (e.g., Faro) operations.

11 Schematic plan of a contorted layer of
lead-zinc mineralization as found in
the Omineca "Metamorphic" Belt.
(Simplified from B.C. Dept. of Mines
Bulletin 57)

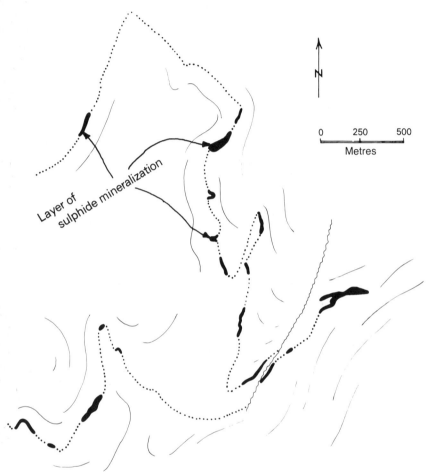

Layer of
sulphide mineralization

N

0   250   500

Metres

In other parts of the Omineca Belt, lead-zinc bearing strata are intensely folded together with the country rock, forming complex ore patterns which are a challenge to both exploration and mining (Figure 11). Many small lead-zinc prospects in the Eastern Belt are concentrated along the boundary between ancient carbonate platforms and thick sequences of shale. Along these facies changes, ore accumulated in a way similar to petroleum: compaction of shale squeezed metal-bearing brines into porous carbonate rocks, where some of the metals precipitated as galena and sphalerite. These occurrences are closely associated with deposits of barite and fluorite, both important industrial minerals.

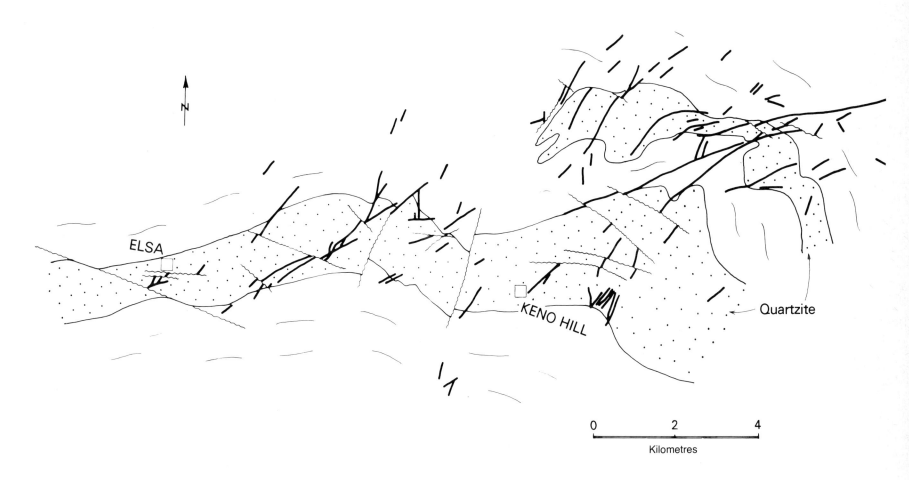

ELSA

KENO HILL

Quartzite

0   2   4

Kilometres

Vein deposits of silver-lead-zinc are the fillings of fractures or faults in the country rock. Metal-bearing solutions invaded the open space during deformation, and quartz, together with specks of sulphide ore, crystallized along the walls. In the Yukon Territory, the silver-lead veins of Keno Hill have yielded rich ore for many years (Figure 12). In British Columbia, the silver veins of the Kootenay Lake, Nelson, and Slocan Camps were mined with great vigour at the turn of the century, when silver was considered second only to gold in value. Often, the initial triumph of the early lode mines gave way to disappointment when the veins lost their pay a few feet below the surface. Now, silver is mainly a byproduct of lead-zinc mining from large stratiform ore bodies.

The first large-scale mining of lead-zinc ores in British Columbia was mainly the result of a technological breakthrough. Through the development of a differential flotation process, the lead, zinc and iron sulphides of the Sullivan Mine could be separated as high-grade concentrates. This, in turn, accounted for the dramatic rise in lead-zinc output from the Trail smelter in the 1920s (Figure 5).

Copper-Molybdenum

No other metal mirrors the changing patterns of human technology as well as copper. Early man retrieved nuggets of pure copper from stream beds and gravel bars to hammer into jewellery and weapons. A small admixture of tin converted copper into bronze, the technological symbol of a European cultural stage in about 1800 B.C. Much later, rich copper ores became an integral part of the monetary and trading empires of medieval Europe.

The biggest boost to the mining of copper came from the invention of electric power. Transmission lines, generators, and batteries devoured copper in an ever-accelerating race between demand and supply which, as yet, shows no sign of slowing down. At the turn of the century, copper ore with 2% copper metal was economical to mine, but now ore grades as low as 0.4% are considered worthwhile for large-scale mining operations. The decline in ore grade has been caused partly by the depletion of richer ore, by rising prices, by technological breakthroughs, and by the discovery of large *porphyry copper* deposits. Molybdenum has come into prominence only recently, as an ingredient of resilient steels. Since deposits of molybdenum are similar to those of copper, and since it is commonly associated with copper in the same deposits, particularly those of the porphyry-type, moybdenum is treated together with copper in this book.

The first European explorers who travelled along the Pacific Coast of British Columbia and Alaska found the natives in possession of copper bracelets, plates, and knives as early as 1741. The Haida people, on the Queen Charlotte Islands, seem to have been the principal traders of copper nuggets, which were said to have come from a copper mountain in the northern interior of the continent. With the arrival of white prospectors in western Canada, regular mining of copper began near Nelson, B.C. There, the veins of the Silver King yielded a rich lode of silver and the ore contained some 20% copper as well. This was in 1888. Soon after, the towns of Rossland and Trail developed out of small but vigorous mining camps, and in 1890 the Rossland camp produced its first ten tons of ore containing gold, silver and copper. This ore had to be packed by mule from Rossland to the Columbia River and then had to be shipped by steamboat and wagon to a smelter in Butte, Montana. From these rather humble beginnings arose the copper mining industry of British Columbia. In subsequent years, the search for copper gave rise to many other camps and towns scattered throughout the rugged and unmapped mountains of British Columbia and the Yukon Territory. At present, copper is the most valuable metal found in western Canada, and the ups and downs of the international copper price have a significant economic impact.

The Canadian Cordillera is only one segment of a copper-molybdenum belt which extends through the Cordilleran mountain chain from Alaska, through Canada, into the western United States, and onward to Mexico, Peru, and Chile. The major copper deposits of British Columbia and the Yukon Territory are scattered throughout the Intermontane Volcanic Belt, but some have also been found in the Coast and Insular Belts (Figure 3).

In many of the early mines of the Canadian Cordillera, copper ore was broken from narrow veins with a copper content as high as 5 to 10%. Vein deposits of copper sulphides, like the veins of other ores, generally did not contain large tonnages of copper, and were soon mined out. Unless larger low-grade mineralization could be tracked down, ghost towns would be all that remained of vein mining. The two types of copper deposits that came into prominence as a result of these exploration efforts were the massive sulphide deposits and the copper porphyries. Copper is also found as an accessory to deposits of almost all other metals, particularly molybdenum, tungsten, and iron. Copper and molybdenum are found most commonly in the form of sulphide minerals, the important ones being brass-yellow chalcopyrite ($CuFeS_2$), iridescent bornite (Cu_5FeS_4), and grey molybdenite (MoS_2). In surface outcroppings, metal-bearing sulphides are often dissolved into yellowish-brown rock stains. Such colourful gossans are valuable guides to the prospector.

13 Horizontal cross-section through the contorted layers of massive copper sulphides at Granduc Mine in northwestern B.C. (Simplified from Canadian Institute of Mining and Metallurgy, Special Volume No. 8)

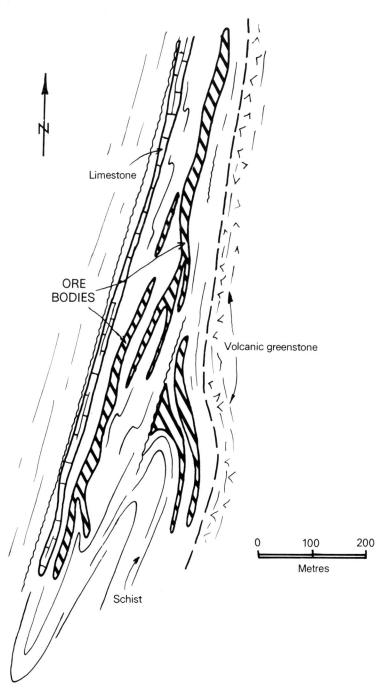

Massive sulphide deposits are tabular or elongate zones of mineralization intimately associated with layers of volcanic greenstones. They always contain significant amounts of gold, silver, and zinc which, by themselves, may extend the life of a mine. Commonly, ore bodies and the enveloping rocks are intricately folded and sheared, making them difficult to predict from surface outcroppings or drill-cores (Figure 13). Important mining centres exist or have existed around the massive sulphide deposits of Western Mines on Vancouver Island, Britannia Beach north of Vancouver and the Anyox-Granduc region of remote northwestern B.C. (Figure 14).

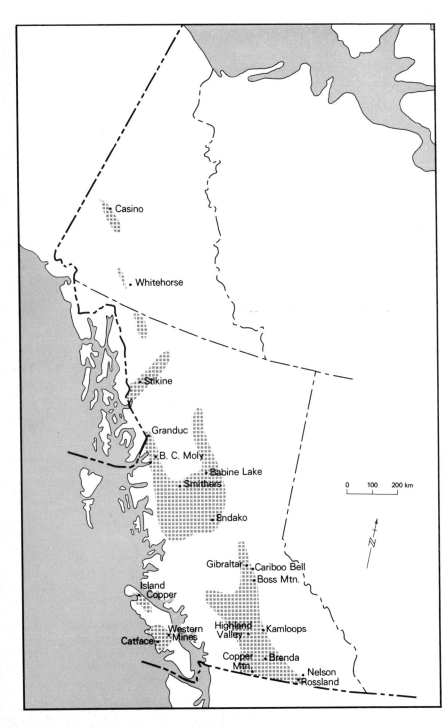

Casino

Whitehorse

Stikine

Granduc

B. C. Moly

Babine Lake

Smithers

Endako

0   100   200 km

N

Gibraltar   Cariboo Bell
             Boss Mtn.

Island
Copper

Western   Highland
Mines   Valley   Kamloops

Catface

Copper   Brenda
Mtn.

Nelson
Rossland

The *copper-molybdenum porphyries* are the real giants among copper deposits and account for the explosive rise of production in western Canada (Figure 15). The word porphyry is Greek in origin and describes the texture of the rock encasing the copper-molybdenum sulphides. A porphyry has large crystals of feldspar or quartz in a fine-grained mass of silicate minerals which crystallized during the intrusion of a batholith into thick volcanic or sedimentary strata. Fracturing of the porphyry and its volcanic envelope opened fissures for the ascent of hot metal-rich brines. The metals precipitated from the brines, along a myriad of fractures within the porphyry or the volcanic host, in the form of sulphides. Within the total mineralized rock volume, the metal grade may well be less than 0.5% copper, 0.15% molybdenum, and 0.2% tungsten. However, the large tonnage makes it feasible to mine the copper porphyries in large open-pit excavations rather than in the more cumbersome underground workings of the past. However, in open-pit mining, huge quantities of rock must be crushed in order to extract the disseminated copper minerals. The waste material discharged from the crusher has to be pumped into carefully retained tailings ponds to prevent the acid rock flour from polluting creeks and lakes in the neighbourhood of mines.

The heartland of the B.C. copper mining industry is the Highland Valley, where several mines are operating or being developed. Mineralization in the Highland Valley occupies fractures in the porphyric rocks of the Guichon Batholith (Figure 16). An important cluster of copper and molybdenum deposits of the porphyry type extends from the Highland Valley across the north-central part of British Columbia, including the Kamloops area, Boss Mountain and Gibraltar, Babine Lake, Endako, and many prospects in the Smithers area. Another region of active exploration straddles the southern border of British Columbia from Vancouver Island to the Okanagan, and includes Island Copper, Copper Mountain, and Brenda Mine. Other porphyry copper showings have been explored or brought into production along a belt of old volcanic rocks extending from the Stikine River northward across the Whitehorse Copper Belt to Casino in the Yukon.

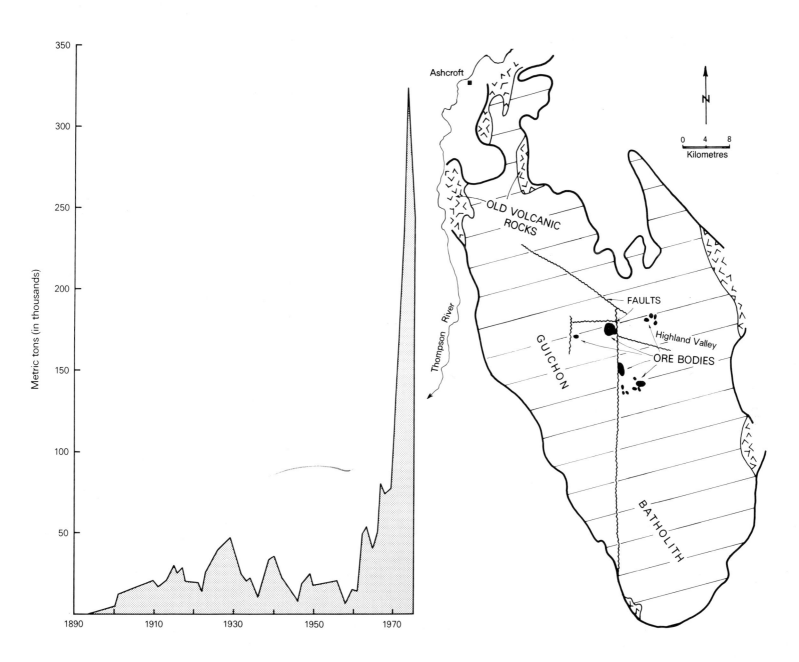

15 Annual production of copper in British Columbia since the beginning of copper mining. The recent peak indicates the production from porphyry-copper mines, followed by a drop in the world price of copper. (Source: B.C. Minister of Mines, annual reports)

16 Map showing the areas of copper mineralization in the Highland Valley, southern B.C. The ore bodies are located in the centre of the Guichon Batholith which intruded volcanic rocks some 200 million years ago.

Ashcroft

OLD VOLCANIC ROCKS

Thompson River

FAULTS

GUICHON

Highland Valley

ORE BODIES

BATHOLITH

N

0   4   8
Kilometres

17 Vertical cross-section through a porphyry-copper deposit in southern B.C. The location of ore bodies with more than 0.3 percent copper and the design of the ultimate open-pit is based on information gained from numerous drill holes. (Simplified from Canadian Institute of Mining and Metallurgy, Volume 66, No. 732)

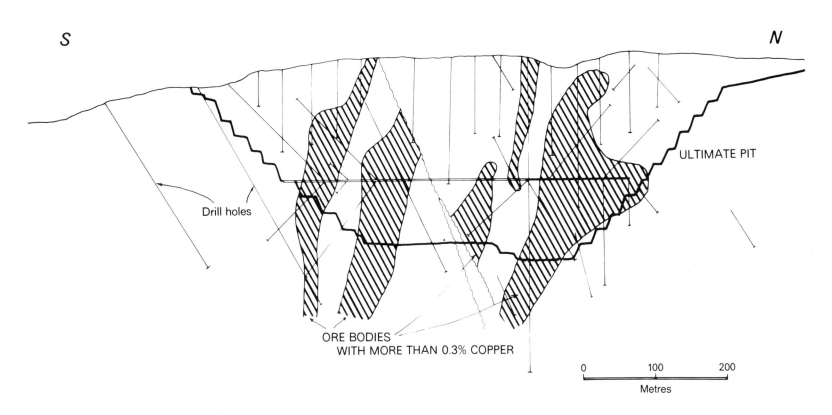

S

N

ULTIMATE PIT

Drill holes

ORE BODIES
WITH MORE THAN 0.3% COPPER

0   100   200

Metres

In the discovery and economic production of porphyry copper, much depends on the drilling of holes and a successful retrieval of drill core to enable the mining engineer to make an estimate of the distribution of copper within a deposit. The pit geometry has to be designed accordingly (Figure 17). Drilling reduces some of the risks of mining and lowers the cost of waste disposal. Therefore, the art of a good drilling program lies in defining the ore bodies as accurately as possible by an economical design of the drill-hole pattern.

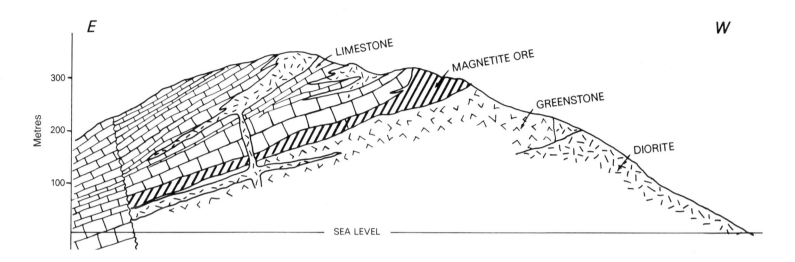

Iron

Iron, on the average, makes up about six per cent of the earth's crust. Because of its relative abundance iron is concentrated in some very large deposits. On a global scale, ore with more than 30% iron is common. The economic feasibility of mining a certain deposit is primarily governed by availability of transportation to the nearest steel works. There, the raw iron ore is converted to steel, the cornerstone of modern engineering.

In British Columbia, iron is found in the Insular Belt, where mining goes back as far as 1885 when iron ores were first worked on Texada Island. Subsequently, iron deposits were discovered on the west coast of the Queen Charlotte Islands (Tasu Sound) and in many smaller prospects scattered throughout Vancouver Island. The iron-bearing mineral in the island deposits is black magnetite (Fe_3O_4—an iron oxide), masses of which replaced limestone or volcanic greenstone when hot intrusions ascended from deep within the earth more than 100 million years ago (Figure 18). This kind of mineral deposit, which formed because crustal rocks had been heated by an intrusion of granite or diorite, is called skarn (an old Swedish miner's term for the coarse and generally well-developed crystal assemblages of this ore type). Copper and other metals are also found in skarn deposits.

The magnetic properties of magnetite have been used to detect concentrations of this mineral, even below a dense cover of vegetation and soil. Air-born magnetometer surveys over ores rich in magnetite show a positive anomaly and may guide the prospector to ore deposits associated with magnetite. However, the largest reserve of iron ore in the Canadian Cordillera is not of the magnetite type, but is a banded iron formation of hematite (Fe_2O_3). This deposit was found in the Mackenzie Mountains, northern Yukon Territory, and contains a huge tonnage of iron ore with 40 to 50% iron. The iron formation is interlayered with the sedimentary strata of the Mackenzie Mountains, and the thin layers of hematite are thought to have been precipitated more than one million years ago at the bottom of the ocean. Although discovered in 1962, this deposit has not yet been developed because of the great distance between the ore body and prospective markets.

Iron is also a byproduct of some copper and lead-zinc deposits in southern British Columbia.

19 Area of important tungsten
mineralization along the border
between the Yukon and Northwest
Territories.

Tungsten

Tungsten is an important ingredient in the manufacture of
cutting tools and tough steels. In the Cordillera of Canada,
tungsten occurs mainly in the Omineca Metamorphic Belt
and the Eastern Belt, where granitic intrusions cut limestone
formations. There, the mineral schelite (WO_3) formed in
skarns.

An important area of tungsten mineralization straddles
the border between the Northwest and Yukon Territories.
Ore bodies are being developed or mined near the townsite
of Tungsten, N.W.T., and MacMillan Pass, Y.T. and N.W.T.
(Figure 19). Similar types of skarn deposits have been
discovered in southeastern B.C., where they are associated
with lead-zinc mineralization. An example of the ore bodies
of tungsten is illustrated in Figure 20, which is a schematic
cross-section through a tungsten mine near Salmo,
southeastern B.C. The complicated geometry of the ore
requires an almost equally complex pattern of shafts, drifts,
and crosscuts to extract it. For the sake of simplicity these
were omitted from the figure. In other parts of the Western
Cordillera, tungsten is a byproduct of the mining of
molybdenum-rich porphyry deposits.

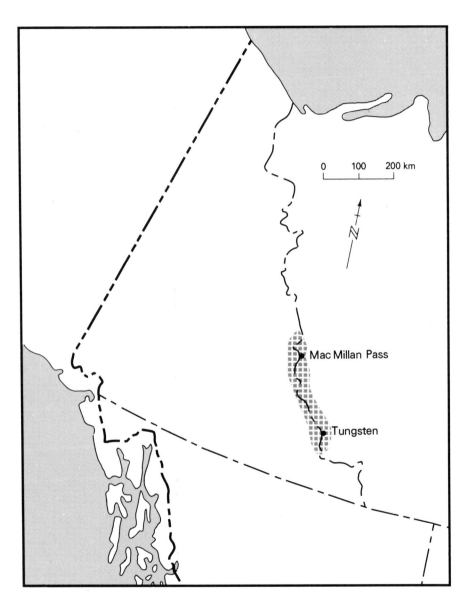

20 Vertical cross-section through a typical tungsten mine in southern B.C. The ore occurs in a 'skarn' which formed when a granitic intrusion altered layers of limestone. For the sake of simplicity, the mine workings are not shown. (Simplified from B.C. Dept. of Mines, *Geology, Exploration and Mining 1973*)

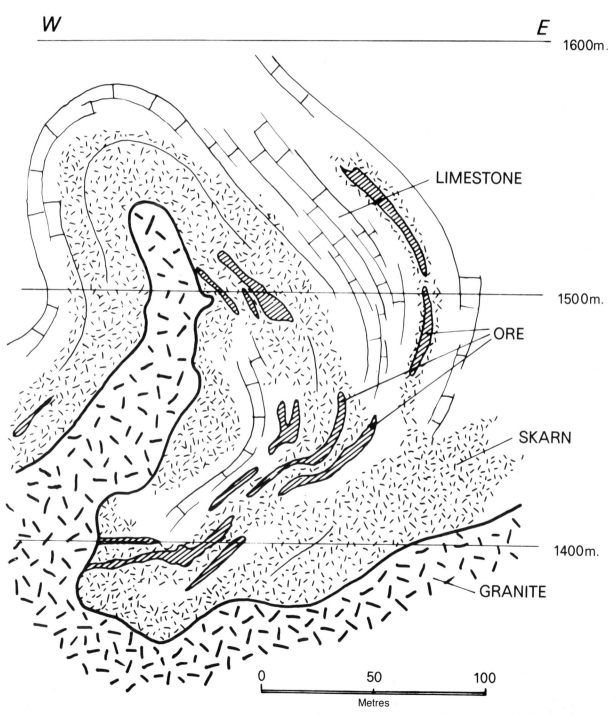

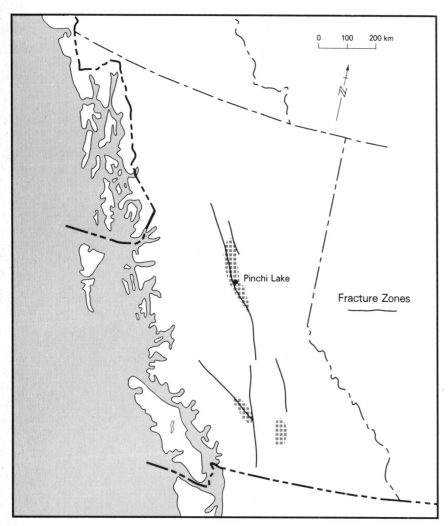

21 Areas known to be favourable for the occurrence of mercury deposits in British Columbia. These seem to be closely related to ancient faults in the earth's crust.

0   100   200 km

Pinchi Lake

Fracture Zones

Mercury

Mercury is essential to modern technology; it is the only metallic substance which is liquid at ordinary temperatures. It is used mainly in precision instruments, electronic gadgets, and explosives. For most of its applications, there is no substitute for mercury.

Mercury is found as the pink earthy mineral, cinnabar (HgS). In British Columbia, deposits are located along zones adjacent to old fractures in the earth's crust in the Intermontane Belt (Figure 21). The most significant mercury showings were discovered in 1937 near Pinchi Lake, north-central B.C., and subsequent mining has been most productive there. Although closed from time to time for economic reasons, the Pinchi Lake Mine has been Canada's only mercury producer for many years. Because of the toxic nature of mercury, all mill water from a mercury mine has to be reused in a closed circuit, and industrial hygiene and environmental controls are of the highest standard.

22 Location of the Cassiar and Clinton
Creek asbestos mines in relation to
the northern transportation routes.

Industrial Minerals and Structural Materials

In addition to metals and fuels, the outer shell of the earth supplies materials for the construction of highways and houses, and for diverse other uses. Large tonnages of these materials are required, and their excavation demands great technical skill and a high level of environmental planning. As in the case of iron resources, the development of large deposits is tied to transportation routes.

Asbestos, a light-green fibrous material made up mainly of the mineral chrysotile ($Mg_3Si_2O_5(OH)_4$), is in great demand because it is fire resistant and a good insulator. Chrysotile formed millions of years ago when fluids passed through magnesium-rich silicate rocks and changed their mineralogy. The result of this alteration is a green rock called serpentinite which contains two principal minerals, chrysotile and magnetite (Fe_3O_4). The association of magnetite with asbestos has often been used successfully to find new occurrences by magnetometer surveys.

The two producers of asbestos fibre in western Canada are at Cassiar, B.C., and Clinton Creek, Y.T. (Figure 22).

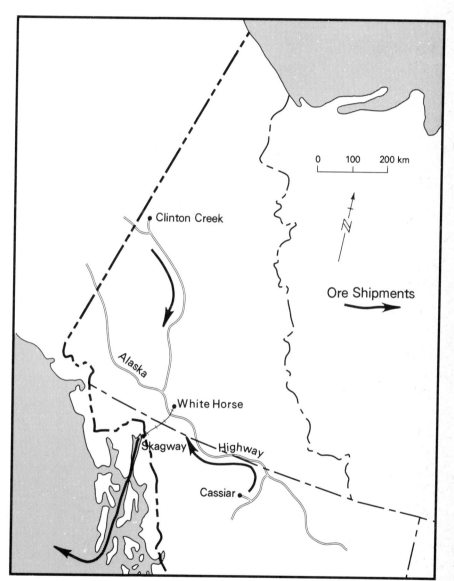

0   100   200 km

Ore Shipments

Clinton Creek

Alaska

White Horse

Skagway

Highway

Cassiar

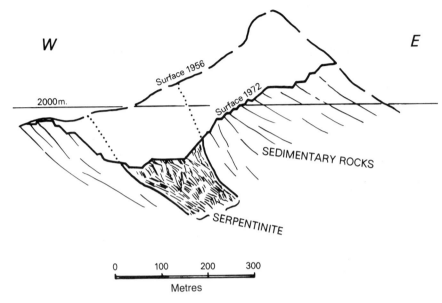

23 Vertical cross-section through the Cassiar asbestos mine where a mountain was removed between 1956 and 1972. The commercially important asbestos occurs within the zone of serpentinite. (Simplified from B.C. Dept. of Mines, *Geology, Exploration and Mining 1972*)

The Cassiar deposit was found in 1950, and since about 1956 a whole mountainside has been gradually lowered by the extraction of asbestos and the removal of overlying waste rock (Figure 23). The discovery and development of both these deposits has been closely linked to the expansion of the northern highway system, particularly the Alaska Highway.

Barite and *fluorite* are industrial minerals which have been sporadically mined in the Omineca and Eastern Belts of the Cordillera. Because of its high specific gravity, barite ($BaSo_4$) is added to paints and various types of mud used in the drilling of oil wells. Fluorite (CaF_2) is used as a flux in the making of steel and is a source of fluorine, which is valued in dental hygiene as well as in chemical industries. Barite and fluorite commonly occur in veins and layers, sometimes closely associated with lead-zinc deposits. Thus far, economically feasible deposits have been located in southeastern British Columbia and the Yukon. *Building stone, cement, clay, shale, limestone, gypsum,* and *gravel* are needed in increasing amounts by the construction industries in and around urban centres. Quarries and pits are therefore dug not simply where the stone is good or the gravel abundant, but preferably close to construction projects. For example, construction projects in the Vancouver and Victoria areas supported limestone quarrying (limestone is the valuable source of cement) on Texada Island for many years.

Distance from active development also controls the location of commercial sand and gravel pits. Some five hundred gravel pits are in operation throughout British Columbia and the Yukon. They serve mostly to extend and maintain the highway system or, temporarily, to supply earth and rock material for domestic and industrial construction.

Growing environmental awareness in the face of rapid urban expansion requires careful management of gravel operations so that the pit can be reclaimed after it has been exhausted. In low-lying regions such as the Lower Mainland area, deep gravel pits are potential conduits for groundwater contaminants, and the dumping of pollutants into abandoned pits must be avoided. Another point to consider in urban areas is a lesson learned the hard way in southern Ontario: often housing developments spread over valuable gravel deposits which are then lost, leading to increased transportation costs for gravel on a regional scale. As in the case of soil and water resources, the extraction of sand and gravel has to be part of a regional land-use plan.

Coal

Coal has been used as a fuel for almost 800 years. It emerged as the principal energy source during the Industrial Revolution, and still holds its own as an important solid fuel and raw material in heavy industry.

Long time-spans of geological history went into the making of the coal seams, which are now broken from rock faces in underground or open-pit mines. Most of the coals in British Columbia and the Yukon Territory originated more than 100 million years ago in lowland swamps, the end product of decaying masses of luxuriant freshwater swamp vegetation. These low-lying tracts of land were near the mouths of large rivers which dumped silt and mud over the decaying trees and leaves. Eventually, subsidence and sediment accumulation caused the burial of many layers of plant material. The increasing load of sand and clay compressed the loose organic material and initiated the slow process of coalification. The first stage in the conversion of plant debris to coal can be studied today in *peat* deposits such as those of the Fraser River delta, where decaying sphagnum moss piles up in layers up to several metres thick.

In ancient delta regions, the burial and compaction of peat resulted in a gradual enrichment of carbon. With this, the peat changed into *lignite*, then into *sub-bituminous* and *bituminous coal*, and finally into *anthracite*, which has the highest carbon content of all coals. This slow geological process was mainly due to the higher temperatures prevailing at greater depths in the earth's crust. As the carbon content of coal rose, water, methane, and oxygen were driven off, thereby increasing the rank of coal. As a rule, the rank of coal depends on the temperatures to which the coal seams had been exposed before they were elevated by uplift of mountain ranges.

24 A general classification of coals with
    respect to their calorific value and
    carbon content.

The heat-producing value of coal increases with its rank; anthracite is foremost (Figure 24). At present, anthracite, sub-bituminous coal, and lignite (thermal coals) are used mainly to drive electric power plants. Bituminous coals (coking coals) are in high demand because they are the raw material for coke, which is necessary in the reduction of iron ore to steel in blast furnaces. To make coke, the bituminous coal is heated in coke ovens, where the volatile matter (methane, etc.) is driven off and a grey porous mass of carbon stays behind. The coke goes to the steel mills, and the gas products are further refined into chemical compounds such as those used by the plastics industry. Because of their significance as coking coals, the bituminous coals are again subdivided into high-volatile, medium-volatile, and low-volatile classes, according to their gas content (Figure 25). Sub-bituminous coal and lignite are not in great demand at present, but will become a significant source of fuel for electric power plants in the near future. Good coal should be low in ash, which means it should not contain detrital admixtures such as silt and clay. Another feature of high-quality coal is a low sulphur content: the burning of high-sulphur coals creates a serious air pollution problem.

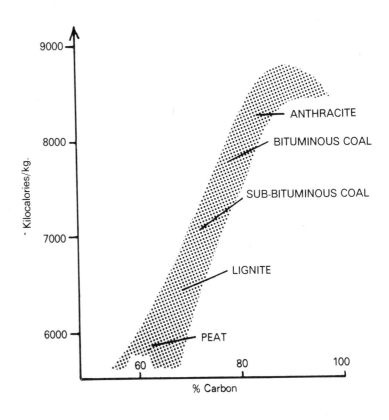

40

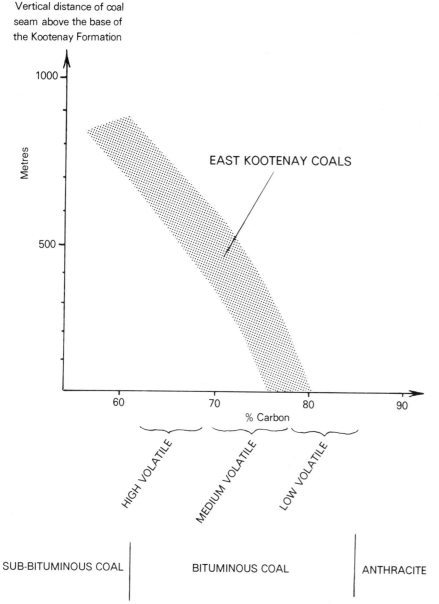

25 Types of coal found in the Kootenay Formation of southeastern B.C. Coals high in the formation have a lower carbon and high gas content. (Generalized from Canadian Institute of Mining and Metallurgy Bulletin Volume 64, No. 714)

Coal mining in the Canadian west began along the east coast of Vancouver Island. From 1835 onward, outcroppings of coal were mined on a local scale; in 1852, mining became an industry when the Hudson's Bay Company took possession of the coal fields in Nanaimo Bay. For the next hundred years, coal was a major economic and political force on the island, only to be replaced by a steadily growing forest industry.

In the Rocky Mountain region, the presence of coal was noted even earlier than on Vancouver Island by explorers traveling upstream into unknown territory. Alexander Mackenzie may have been the first to record smouldering coal seams along the banks of the Peace River when he concluded his diary entry for May 20, 1793: "… Mr. Mackay informed me, that in passing over the mountains, he observed several chasms in the earth that emitted heat and smoke, which diffused a strong sulphurous stench. I should certainly have visited this phenomenon, if I had been sufficiently qualified as a naturalist, to have offered scientific conjectures or observations thereon." In Mackenzie's time, however, fur was king, and the coals of the Peace River canyon lay undisturbed for more than a century.

26 Annual production of coal in British
Columbia from the beginning of
coalmining. The first peak around
1910 indicates the railroad boom; the
second marks the development of
coking coal for export to Japan.
(Source: B.C. Minister of Mines,
annual reports)

Only the westward advance of railroads laid the groundwork for coal mining in the Eastern Belt. In the 1950s, the railroads switched from coal to diesel fuel; as a consequence, the coal industry of the Kootenays fell into a temporary slump, but was rejuvenated by the renewed interest in coking coal. This most recent wave of activity, dating from the late 1960s, is directed toward large-scale extraction of coking coal to be used almost entirely by the steel mills and base-metal smelters of energy-deficient Japan (Figure 26). In the future, coking coal from western Canada may also be shipped to the steel mills of eastern Canada.

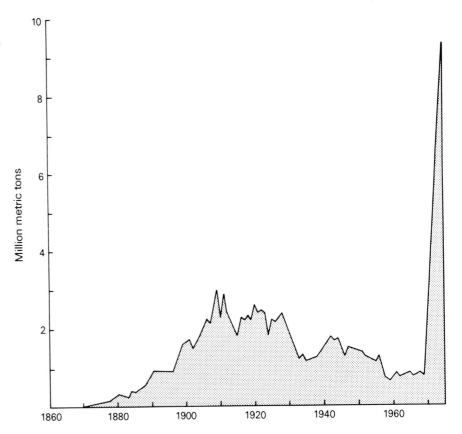

27 Outline of the principal coal-bearing
formations of eastern British Columbia
and other localities of interest in the
past and future development of coal
resources.

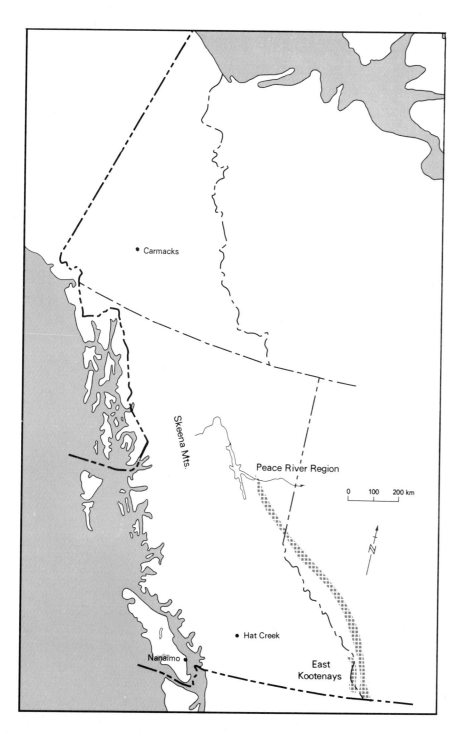

The principal coal resources of British Columbia are the low- to medium-volatile bituminous coals of the Eastern Belt (Figure 27). The sub-bituminous coals of Vancouver Island, which fueled many homes, locomotives, and steamships of the past, are mined out. The two regions in the Eastern Belt with the greatest reserves of coal are the East Kootenay and Peace River districts. They are part of the Rocky Mountain coal belt that extends from northern B.C. through Alberta into the western United States. Although the choice of mining techniques in these districts depends greatly on the rock structure which encloses the coal, most of it can be extracted in open-pit mines along the mountain side. The coal seams in this region may vary in thickness from two to ten metres over short distances, and some thick seams split into several thinner ones. These and other problems, such as folding and faulting of the rock strata, are major challenges in the design of an efficient mining operation.

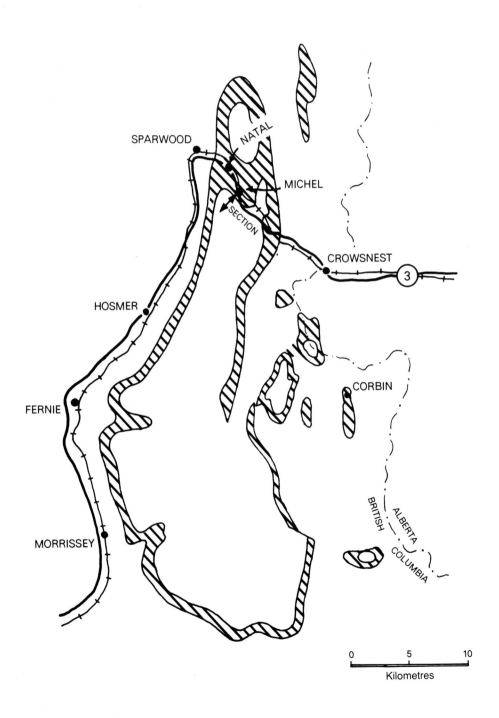

28 Sketch map of the coal-bearing Kootenay Formation near the border between British Columbia and Alberta.

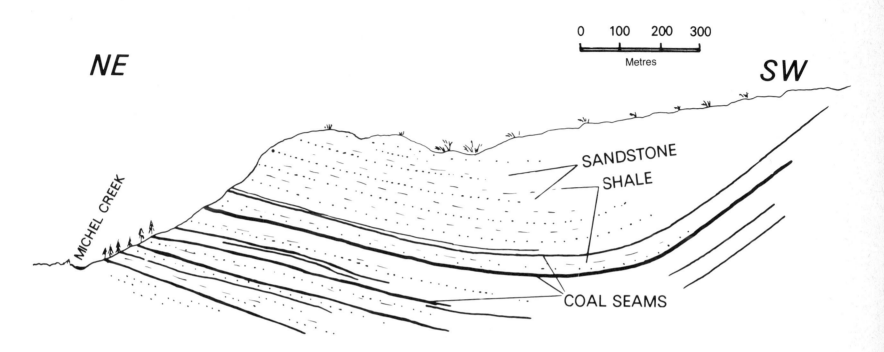

29 A vertical cross-section through the coal-bearing Kootenay Formation near Natal, B.C. The structure of the coal seams is generally very simple. (Simplified from B.C. Dept. of Mines Bulletin 33)

NE

SW

0   100   200   300
Metres

MICHEL CREEK

SANDSTONE

SHALE

COAL SEAMS

In the East Kootenay, the coal seams are lodged in the sandstones and shales of the Kootenay Formation, which is about 1,000 metres thick and commonly contains more than ten coal seams stacked on top of each other. Figure 28 shows the outcrops of the Kootenay Formation within the regional structure called the Fernie Basin. Coal rank varies from seam to seam in the Kootenay Formation, because individual seams were at different depths before they were uplifted and deformed by mountain building some 50 million years ago. The coal rank is higher near the base than farther up the section (Figure 25), and the formation is gently tilted (Figure 29).

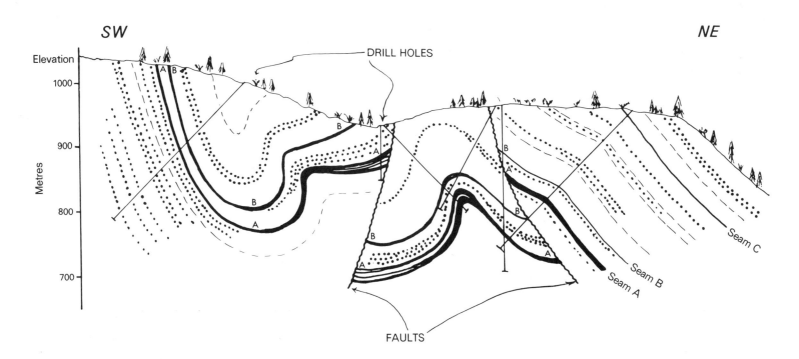

30 Vertical cross-section through coal-bearing strata of northeastern British Columbia. The structure of the coal seams is complicated by folding and faulting of the strata. To ascertain subsurface conditions, drill holes are used to correlate seams such as A and B. (Simplified from B.C. Dept. of Mines Bulletin 36)

In the Peace River and Sukunka River regions of northeastern British Columbia, coal is found mainly within the Gething Formation. The coal seams in this region are commonly folded or broken by faults (Figure 30). The structure can be determined by geologic mapping and drilling, and a suitable mining method can then be chosen to meet the natural geologic conditions.

Although much of the future extraction of coal will be done in the Eastern Belt, some coal will also be produced from the smaller occurrences in the Intermontane Belt. One such sedimentary basin, the Tantalus Mine near Carmacks (Yukon Territory), has been a local supplier of coal since the territory was opened up during the Klondike gold rush. It is now used to dry lead-zinc concentrates at the nearby Anvil Mine (Faro). Other deposits, such as the Hat Creek lignite field near Lillooet and coal showings in the Skeena Mountains of northwestern B.C., will become economically important in the future, when coals will have to be used to a greater extent than at present to meet coming energy deficiencies.

Modern open-cast mining of coal has given a new life to many communities in the East Kootenay. Surface mining has also eliminated most of the hazards the traditional miner had to face underground. However, the gigantic cuts into the coal-bearing mountain sides have created a new set of problems and have put considerable pressure on the new operators to maintain a satisfactory level of environmental standards in the control of drainage, the revegetation of waste dumps, and in the stability of natural slopes. Landslides in waste dumps are undesirable not only because of their effect on drainage but also because they interfere with the operation of the mine itself. In underground mining, the dramatic expansion of scale has led to many new techniques such as hydraulic mining of coal, which uses the pressure of a water jet to break up the coal seams.

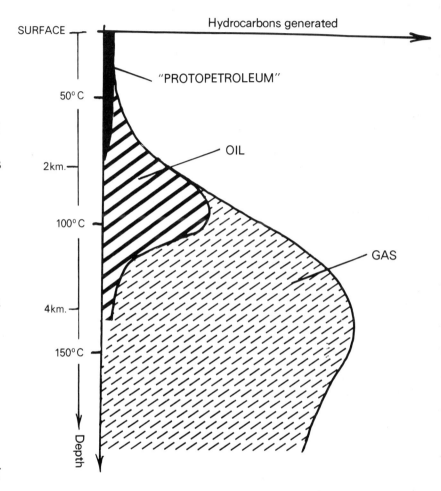

Oil and Gas

The great advantage of oil and gas over other fuels is that the production, transportation and use are relatively simple. Solid fuels such as uranium and coal require complex mining techniques, transport, and refining systems before they are ready for the market. Oil and gas, when drilled in sufficient quantity to warrant economic extraction, are simply pumped from drill holes to processing plants, and on to refineries and industrial centres which produce everything from diesel fuels to pantyhose and headache pills. The diversity of products, particularly those derived from gas, reflects our overwhelming dependence on hydrocarbons to support our present lifestyle.

The raw energy which now fuels a great part of the world's economy has been captured from the rays of the sun by small organisms through the process of photosynthesis. The sedimentation of trillions of tiny organisms at the bottom of the sea and their subsequent burial and biochemical degradation were the initial stages of petroleum formation. During the early steps of this process, the tissues of microscopic plants and animals were converted to dense organic molecules. These organic mixtures are called *kerogen* or *protopetroleum*. Over millions of years, under a mounting load of sediment and an increasing temperature, this substance was gradually cracked into lighter hydrocarbon compounds: the liquids were liberated first, followed later by the gases (Figure 31). During compaction of the clay particles around the small droplets and pockets of petroleum, oil and gas, together with interstitial saltwater, were squeezed from the source rock and began to migrate into more porous reservoir rocks such as sandstones or ancient carbonate reefs. There, the oil and gas were stopped from further migration by impermeable barriers such as well-compacted layers of shale. This is essentially the mechanism that creates the pools which are the target of petroleum exploration.

In searching for pools of gas and oil, the petroleum geologist needs a thorough understanding of the rock structure far below the surface of the earth, and a feeling for where porous rock formations are to be expected within a generally petroliferous region. One of the best techniques used to obtain this knowledge is seismic exploration; crews test the ground by transmitting elastic waves through it and measuring their travel time. This information is then converted into educated guesses concerning the nature of the layering and the rock types involved in the subsurface. However, the real test is the drilling of an exploratory well. Despite great advances in oil exploration, it is still common to find that a promising rock structure yields nothing but a discouraging number of dry holes.

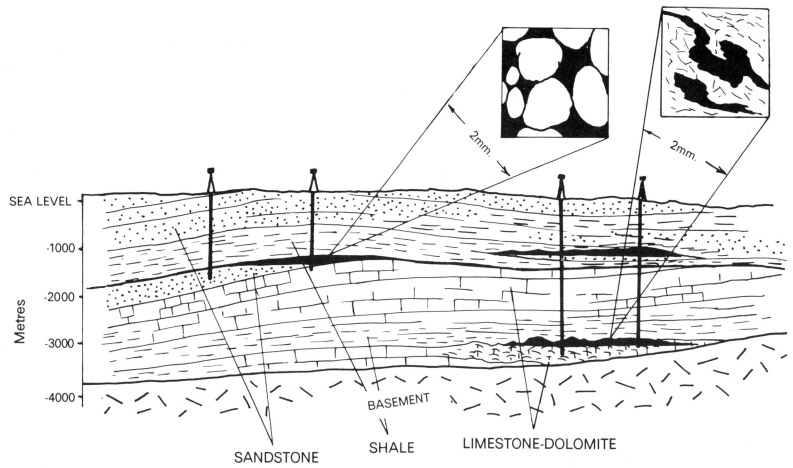

32 Schematic vertical cross-section through the oil and gas fields of northeastern British Columbia. The petroleum occurs in porous rock formations commonly sealed by layers of shale. Insets indicate that petroleum (shaded black) fills the pore space between grains of sandstone or small cavities in dolomite and limestone.

The presence of oil and gas in any sedimentary basin, therefore, depends on a source rock rich in organic matter, a porous formation into which the hydrocarbons migrated, and an impervious barrier that blocked the migration of petroleum and caused the accumulation of a pool.

More than sixty per cent of the world's known reserves of oil and gas are lodged in the basins of the Middle East. Canada has only two to three per cent of the world total, with British Columbia and the Yukon contributing a small fraction of this percentage. The potential for oil and gas in western Canada was known for many years before the first commercial wells were drilled, but the actual development of

the petroleum resources was stepped up only after World War II. The plains and foothills of northeastern British Columbia are part of the Western Canadian Sedimentary Basin, which consists of strata of sandstone, shale and carbonate rock, floored by a crystalline basement. This basement (at a depth of about 4,000 metres below sea-level) is the lower limit of oil and gas exploration (Figure 32). Although drilling for petroleum in northeastern British Columbia goes back to 1921, the first major commercial well was brought into production near Fort St. John in 1952. In British Columbia, the major fields were found to be similar to those discovered and developed a few years earlier in adjacent Alberta.

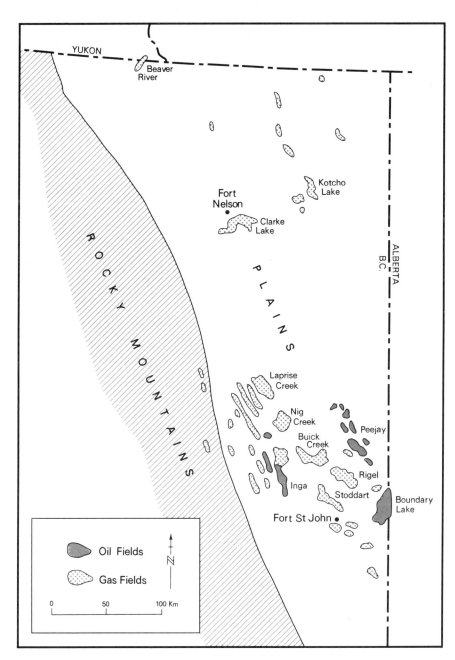

33 Location of the principal oil and gas fields in northeastern British Columbia (after B.C. Dept. of Mines and Petroleum Resources, 1973)

YUKON

Beaver River

Kotcho Lake

Fort Nelson

Clarke Lake

ROCKY MOUNTAINS

PLAINS

ALBERTA B.C.

Laprise Creek

Nig Creek

Peejay

Buick Creek

Rigel

Inga

Stoddart

Boundary Lake

Fort St John

Oil Fields

Gas Fields

N

0   50   100 Km

The development of gas and oil resources is generally preceded by compiling existing geological information and by leasing land from the government for the purpose of seismic sounding and exploratory drilling. If exploration drilling is successful, further drilling must be conducted to appraise the extent of a petroleum field and to define the geometry of individual pools. In British Columbia, about 3,500 wells have been drilled in the search for and development of hydrocarbons; less than half of these have become producers. The total drilling distance in all of these wells is about 5,000 kilometres (roughly the distance between the Atlantic and Pacific Oceans).

The oil and gas of British Columbia is lodged within pores and interstices of ancient carbonate platforms and sand banks buried beneath younger shales and sandstones (Figure 32). The age of these rocks ranges from 500 to 100 million years, and petroleum may have migrated into some of the pools more than 100 million years ago, after it was squeezed from shales rich in organic material.

The typical petroleum pools found in northeastern British Columbia lie between 1,000 and 3,000 metres below the surface (Figure 33). Oil is encountered at shallower levels than gas. The petroleum pumped to the surface is always a mixture of hydrocarbons such as methane, ethane, propane, pentane, benzene, etc., and other elements such as nitrogen, oxygen, and sulphur. Gas is the most important hydrocarbon extracted at present in British Columbia (Figure 34). Methane (CH_4) is the dominant compound of natural gas. *Wet gas* contains oil vapour; *sweet gas* carries small amounts of water; and *sour gas* has a percentage of sulphur in the form of H_2S. Sulphur, now a valuable byproduct collected in the cleaning process of gas, is used by the pulp and fertilizer industries.

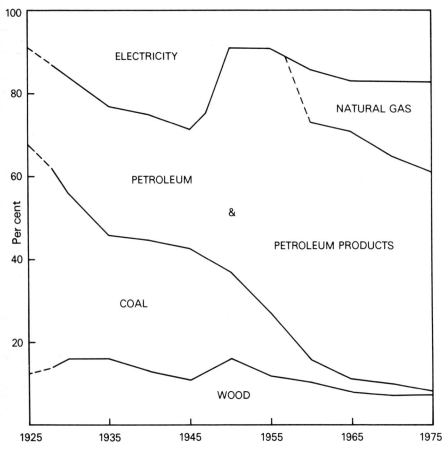

34 Changes in the relative importance of wood, coal, petroleum, natural gas and electricity in the energy supply of British Columbia and Yukon Territory, 1930-1975. (Sources: Statistics Canada Catalogue 57-207 and *Transactions of Second Resources Conference*, Victoria, 1949)

A single gas or oil field may be made up of several pools at different levels and in different rock formations. The pools are outlined by drilling through them and by recording the thickness of the pay zone of oil or gas. Once the discovery well and a few development wells are drilled through the reservoir, a proper spacing of production wells is designed to utilise the natural pressures in the pool for efficient depletion of the field. As an example, Figure 35 shows the outline of the Beaver River gas field on the B.C.-Yukon border, northwest of Fort Nelson. The contours on the map describe the thickness of the gas pay zone within the porous dolomite formation that hosts the gas pool. The geological cross-section shows that, in this case, the impermeable seal is an overlying shale formation; the lower boundary of the gas accumulation is a gas-water interface about 4,000 metres below the surface. The gas reservoir of the Beaver River Field lies in a distinctly arched rock structure, an anticline, which formed during the uplift of the Rocky Mountains some 50 million years ago. Near the Rocky Mountain Foothills, petroleum fields commonly congregate near anticlines; in the plains, they occur in essentially flat-lying strata.

Although exploration for petroleum has centred mainly around the known fields of the Western Canadian Sedimentary Basin and its northward extension, some effort has gone into finding hydrocarbons elsewhere. In the northern Yukon Territory recent exploration has encountered several promising areas, but exploitation will depend on new discoveries there and in the adjacent Mackenzie Delta of the Northwest Territories. Only a sufficiently large quantity of gas or oil justifies the building of a pipeline to consumers in southern Canada.

A few exploration wells have also been drilled in the off-shore area of the Insular Belt of British Columbia and in the sedimentary basins of the Intermontane Belt. Thick sedimentary strata were indicated by geological mapping and seismic surveys, but subsequent drilling has been disappointing.

Gas is a precious commodity. In the future, it may become too precious to serve as a substitute for other fuels. Some quantity of gas will be extracted from coal, but the cost of coal gas promises higher prices for fertilizers, synthetic fibres, and paints.

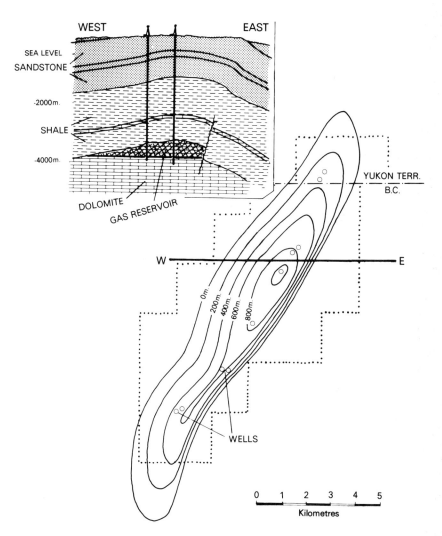

36 A: Schematic plan of a hydro-electric
site; B: Vertical cross-section from the
power intake to the tailrace tunnel;
C: Cross-section through a rock-fill
dam.

Hydro-electric Power

Hydro-electric energy is the harnessed power of water rushing from springs and lakes high in the mountains to the sea. The height through which water falls in any particular stretch of a river determines the potential energy available for power generation. This potential energy is converted into mechanical energy by means of turbines which, in turn, drive generators capable of producing electricity.

The simplest and oldest form of obtaining electric power from running water is a *run-of-river* installation, in which part of a river is slightly diverted from its natural course and directly channeled onto turbines. In most mountainous areas such as the Canadian Cordillera, the runoff carried by the rivers fluctuates considerably with the seasons. The ratio of the highest recorded runoff (spring melt or fall rains) to the lowest stage of a river (summer drought and winter freeze-up) on the Fraser River is 70:1, on the Skeena 100:1. The irregularity of the power source is, therefore, a distinct disadvantage of run-of-river installations. Another disadvantage is the small vertical drop of the natural riverbed, which severely limits the amount of power that can be produced.

To overcome these difficulties, most hydro sites in mountainous terrain involve the construction of dams whereby large reservoirs of water are impounded. This controls the timing of runoff according to need. Moreover, when a high dam is built across a valley, the vertical drop between the surface of the lake above the dam and the turbines below it greatly exceeds the drop of the river in its natural state. This vertical drop or head of a storage reservoir and the quantity of water available determine the capacity of a hydro-electric installation. Large dams raise both the head and the quantity of water available, thus increasing the capacity of the installation. The capacity is expressed in kilowatts; the actual energy produced during a certain time interval is recorded in kilowatt hours (kwh).

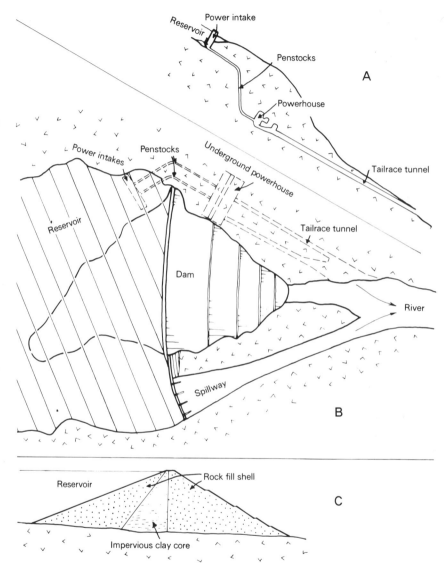

37 Distribution of major hydro-electric
installations in British Columbia and
Yukon Territory.

To obtain a large and high storage reservoir, narrow canyons are closed by concrete shells, wider valleys by large dams of rock and earth. Several elements are present in most hydro-electric installations. The essential ones are shown in Figure 36. From the reservoir impounded by a dam, the water surges through the intake towers, down the penstocks, and onto the turbines which are installed in a powerhouse; it leaves the site through the tailrace. During exceptional high water levels, some of the reservoir water may be discharged through a spillway.

Thus, abundant precipitation and high mountains are favourable factors for hydro power generation. British Columbia and the Yukon Territory are blessed with high mountain ranges and deeply incised rivers whose power potential was recognized as soon as mining and industry advanced into the interior of the Cordillera (Figure 37).

The first hydro-electric plant was built along the spectacular Bonnington Falls of the Kootenay River in 1897. This plant and others nearby served the mines of Rossland and later the smelters at Trail. Meanwhile, the growing towns of Victoria and Vancouver also supplemented their small thermal installations with hydro-electric plants, making use of mountain streams in the vicinity (Goldstream River near Victoria, Lake Buntzen drainage near Vancouver). Soon, hydro-electric power generation greatly outstripped the amount of power generated by coal-fired steam plants (Figure 38). The head of the early hydro sites was more or less that of the height of natural waterfalls, and water rushed through intake piers directly onto power-generating turbines. Later, dams were built above natural waterfalls to raise the head, but the early dams were rarely more than a few metres high.

From these humble beginnings, hydro-electric power production grew steadily until about 1950. The growth in population and industrial activity in the Lower Mainland of B.C., the mining centres of the Interior, and logging towns on Vancouver Island were the main stimulants for this increase in development. The level of several lakes north of Vancouver was raised, and tunnels were blasted through the

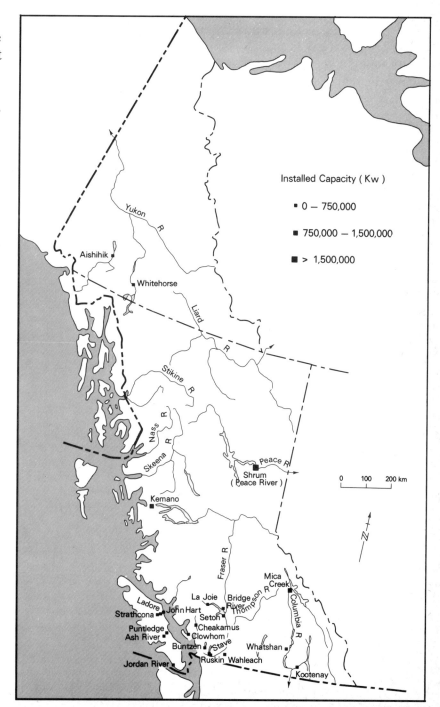

53

38 Growth of energy supplied by
hydro-electric installations and
thermal-power plants in British
Columbia, 1920-1975. (Sources:
Statistics Canada Catalogue 57-001,
57-202 and *Canada Year book,*
annual)

hard bedrock of the Coast Mountains to connect the raised lakes with power houses near sea level. An old report noted, rather romantically, "that the design of Powerhouse No. 2 [Lake Buntzen] was carefully studied from an architectural point of view, and its massive proportions harmonize with the precipitous mountains which form the background."

By about 1950, considerations of harmony with nature had become a minor concern, as power generation was stepped up dramatically (Figure 38). The mileage of transmission lines surged accordingly, and heavy industry, such as the aluminum smelter near Kitimat-Kemano and the lead-zinc smelter of Trail were closely tied to new hydro sites. A similar relationship existed between the forest industry and hydro developments on Vancouver Island. The 1960s and 70s saw the construction of gigantic damsites on the Columbia and Peace Rivers. In comparison with the projects of Kemano-Kitimat, the Columbia-Kootenay and the Peace River, all other hydro-electric projects in the Cordillera are insignificant in their contribution to overall capacity. The three sites of Mica Creek, Peace River, and Kemano-Kitimat alone are able to produce more than two-thirds of the electric energy required. Small installations such as those providing light and heat to municipalities from Whitehorse, Y.T., to Nelson, B.C., are merely the proverbial drop in the bucket. As in mining and logging, the importance of a few large operations now outweighs the significance of the many small ones.

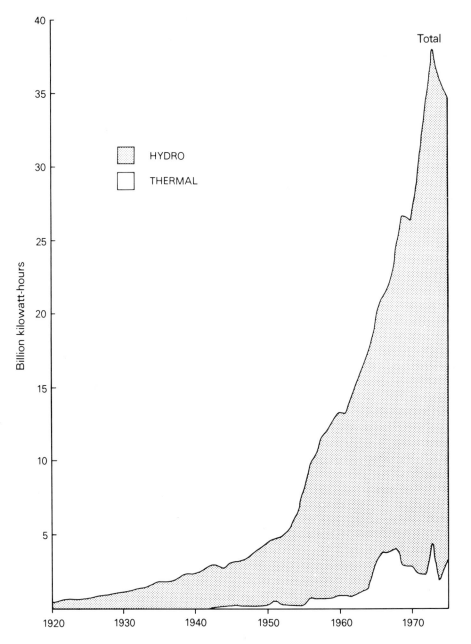

The large dams have created huge lakes. These lakes have raised serious questions as to the quality of the future environment of western Canada. Four points dominate the discussion.

1. In the mountainous regions of B.C. and the Yukon Territory, valley bottoms are generally the only suitable place for permanent human settlement and agriculture. Do people want to lose these areas forever?

2. Most of the large rivers flowing toward the Pacific are valued for their salmon runs (e.g., Fraser, Skeena) and large dams would certainly diminish this resource substantially.

3. Rivers such as the Yukon are now part of the historical heritage of Canada. Many of the pioneer events and lifestyles were related to river travel. Many Canadians retrace the steps of early native hunters, voyageurs, and goldseekers along the rivers of western Canada. Are people willing to drown this heritage?

4. Rarely is forest land logged completely from the site of the future reservoir before it is being impounded. It takes hundreds of years for the waterlogged standing trees to rot away and, thus, they create a menace to potential recreational boaters.

The question arising from all these points is: does it pay to develop another large power site at the cost of losing a valley or a river and their contained resources?

39 The amount of water used daily in
British Columbia and the Territories.
(Source: Environment Canada,
Canada Water Year Book 1975)

Water Resources

Many people assume that there is an ample supply of water for every conceivable purpose. While this is true in some areas, many rivers are subject to extreme fluctuations in flow. A single area may be exposed to both flood and drought within the same year. Thus, despite the large total supply, water is not always available when and where it is needed.

The mountains of western Canada provide some of the widest variations in precipitation imaginable, ranging from 600 centimetres a year on the western slopes of Vancouver Island to 18 centimetres in the southern Interior. Excessive seasonal precipitation and snowmelt can lead to devastating floods. Hot summers may be accompanied by critical periods of low stream flow. Because of these regional and seasonal variations, a real problem arises as soon as local water demand exceeds the supply.

Freshwater is needed for domestic and industrial water supplies, mining (washing and processing of ore), irrigation, and livestock watering (Figures 39 and 40). Some of these activities consume very large quantities of water. For example, the production of one ton of pulp requires from 150,000 to 240,000 litres of water. A pulp mill with a capacity of 500 tons a day withdraws more than 90 million litres of water a day; this is equivalent to 100,000 domestic users.

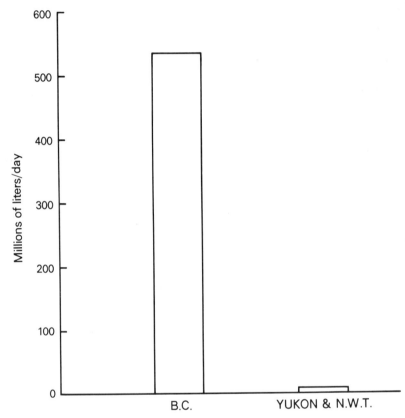

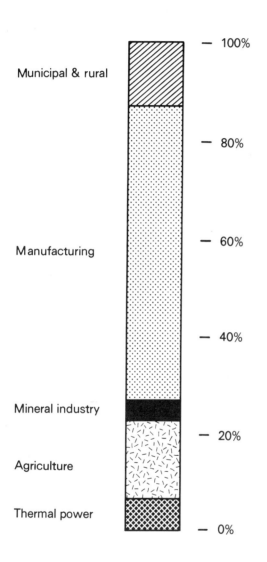

Municipal & rural

Manufacturing

Mineral industry

Agriculture

Thermal power

— 100%

— 80%

— 60%

— 40%

— 20%

— 0%

Of course, not all of the water withdrawn from rivers, lakes or reservoirs is consumed. For example, most of the water in pulp production is also put to work in the debarking of saw-logs and the cooling of engines, but such water is often returned to the environment in an altered, polluted state. Water used for irrigation and other agricultural purposes is generally lost through evapo-transpiration. There are other competitors for water which are non-consumptive: fisheries (the spawning and rearing of salmon), hydro-electric power, and recreation (swimming, boating). To a certain extent, all demands can be met at present, but experience elsewhere is a warning that water resources can be overtaxed. There are limits to the amount of water that can be shared among growing and competing uses, particularly when these activities are concentrated in urban-industrial centres. Not all of these demands are compatible, and the discharge of polluted water into rivers and lakes severely restricts its uses further downstream.

Surface water is often the first to be tapped for domestic and industrial supply, because it is more accessible than groundwater. More than ninety per cent of the water used in British Columbia and the Yukon comes from rivers, lakes and reservoirs. The remaining ten per cent is groundwater drawn from wells. In many areas, the use of groundwater is limited by its high mineral content, but a number of towns and many cottages depend almost totally on wells for their water supply.

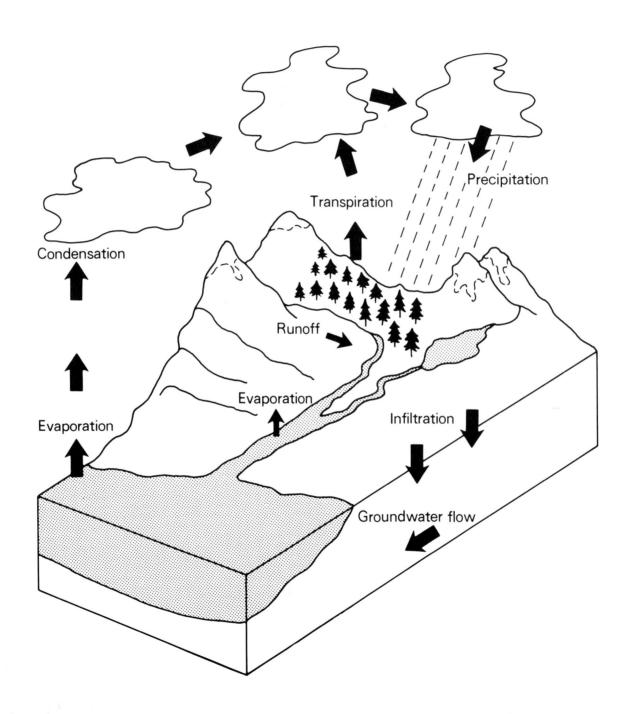

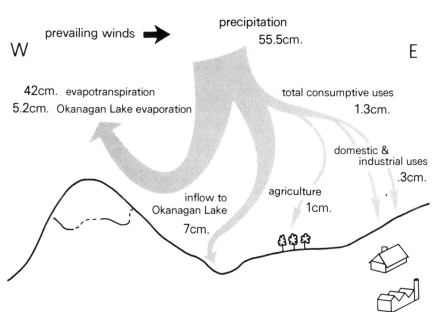

prevailing winds ➡

W

precipitation
55.5cm.

E

42cm. evapotranspiration
5.2cm. Okanagan Lake evaporation

total consumptive uses
1.3cm.

domestic &
industrial uses
.3cm.

inflow to
Okanagan Lake
7cm.

agriculture
1cm.

Surface water and groundwater are closely bound together. Rain and snow which falls over the land may run off in rivulets and creeks. Some, however, infiltrates the soil to form groundwater. On its way to the sea, water evaporates from the surface of streams and lakes (Figures 41 and 42). Of the water which enters the ground, either by direct infiltration or through the banks of beds of streams, part is stored near the surface where it is taken up by vegetation and returned to the atmosphere as the plants transpire. This sequence from cloud to land, to river, to ocean and back to cloud is called the hydrological cycle. In the Cordilleran region, about eighty per cent of the water in the cycle runs off in streams and rivers to the ocean. The remaining twenty per cent is stored as snowpack or groundwater, or is lost by evapotranspiration (Figure 43).

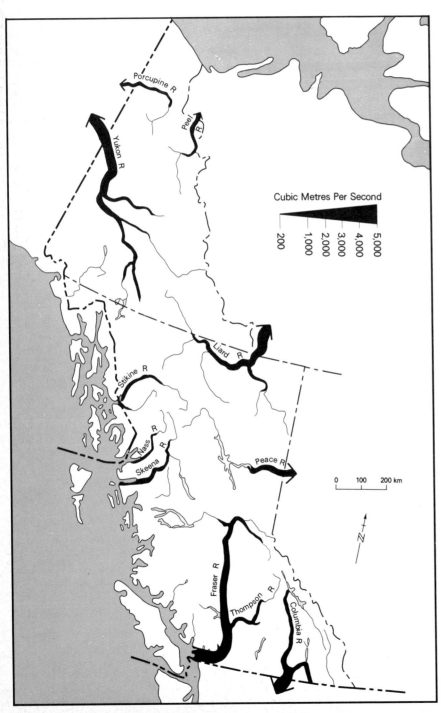

Surface Water

Much of the usable surface water is stored in lakes and
artificial reservoirs or as snowpack in the high mountain
ranges, but most important for sustained use is the volume of
water flowing in streams and rivers (Figure 43). Regional
trends in surface runoff largely reflect precipitation and
storage in snowpack. The seasonal fluctuation in
precipitation and snowmelt causes high freshets in late
spring and low stream flows in midwinter (Figure 44). Such
seasonal and regional variations in the amount of water
available have acted as an incentive to build reservoirs,
divert streams and protect watersheds in order to control
runoff. However, some of the larger projects have other less
beneficial side effects. The construction of sizable dams (and
proposals for more) along rivers such as the Columbia,
Fraser, Yukon, and Peace are lively issues at the present
time. With the exception of the Peace, the rivers of northern
British Columbia and the Yukon Territory remain almost
untouched; development is limited to water supply and
hydro-electric installations supplying local communities.
The rivers of the south have been harnessed to a much
greater extent, supplying the electric power for urban and
industrial development.

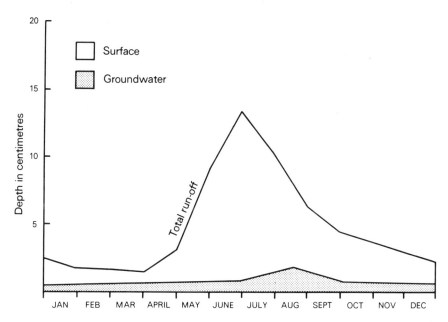

44 The monthly pattern of surface runoff and groundwater flow in the Canadian Cordillera. (Simplified from Geological Survey of Canada, Economic Geology Report No. 24)

The Columbia River ranks fourth in North America in terms of runoff, following the Mississippi, the St. Lawrence, and the Mackenzie. It rises in Columbia Lake and flows northwest before turning south to cross the international boundary on its way to the Pacific Ocean. It flows through Canada for almost half of its total length of 1,640 kilometres. The Kootenay River is its major tributary in Canada. Another is the Pend d'Oreille, which rises in the United States and crosses briefly into Canada before joining the Okanagan River, which flows from Okanagan Lake southward across the border. Runoff in the drainage basin of the Columbia reflects the widely ranging climatic conditions in the region. The high mountains receive most of their precipitation as snow in winter. Rapid melting of the snowpack, sometimes in combination with heavy rainfall, used to create severe floods during May and June.

In 1944, Canada and the United States began a study of ways to increase low winter flows and at the same time reduce spring floods downstream. After two decades of study and negotiation, the Columbia River Treaty was signed in 1964. Canada agreed to build three storage reservoirs to regulate flows for power generation and flood control. In turn, the United States agreed to provide Canada with half of the extra power generated by their hydro plants, and to pay Canada for flood control benefits. At the request of British Columbia, Canada's share of the additional power was sold in advance to utilities in the United States. The three reservoirs have since been completed; the third and largest, Mica, was finished in 1973 (Figure 45). The treaty also gave the U.S. the right to develop the Libby Dam Project on the Kootenay River in Montana. This project, also completed, provides flood control downstream on the Kootenay, as well as hydro-electric power. The Columbia project has come under heavy criticism since the treaty was signed. Some engineers have claimed that the three dams would not make the best use of the available land and the flow characteristics of the river. Economists have suggested that there would have been better ways to obtain the benefits claimed for the treaty. Some of the tributaries of the Columbia River had been dammed in earlier times to provide power for the mining and smelting operations in the Kootenays. Concern is growing that there will be few free-flowing streams left unharnessed, if other projects proposed for this region are given approval.

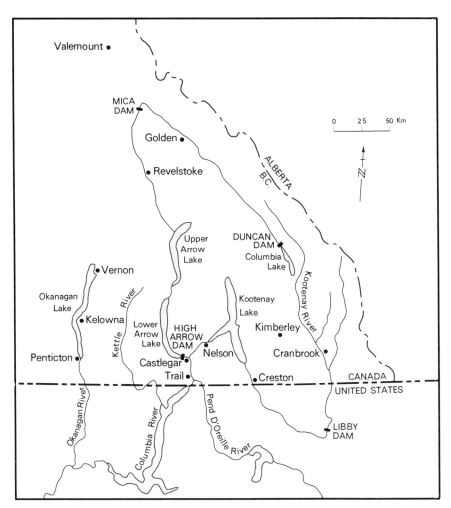

The Fraser River played a vital role in the development of British Columbia and, in the days of the fur traders, provided a transportation route to the Interior of the province. Today, its fertile floodplain, stretching some 130 kilometres inland from the Strait of Georgia, has developed as the major urban-industrial centre of the province. However, the floods which built this fertile region have also posed a serious threat to its economy. The areas most susceptible to frequent and damaging floods are the very areas most attractive for farming and urban development. The major threat of flooding returns every spring, when heavy rainfall combines with rapid snowmelt during unusually warm spells: severe floods hit the lower Fraser valley in 1894, 1948, and 1950. The 1948 flood drowned 22,000 hectares of farmland and left 2,000 people homeless. The total damage is unknown, but $20 million was paid in compensation for flood losses. In response to this disaster, the existing dyke protection was strengthened and expanded. A ten-year, federal-provincial programme was set up in 1968 to improve the river and sea dykes, bank protection, and pumping facilities. However, if a flood larger than the 1948 one occurs in the future, some of the dykes would not hold and there would be extensive damage.

In an attempt to reduce some of the risk, a floodplain policy was adopted in 1973 prohibiting any construction close to the banks of the Fraser River. Dams as a means of regulating the flow for flood control and hydro-electric power on the main stem of the Fraser River had been proposed as early as 1963. This scheme has always met with strong opposition, because it would probably destroy the largest sockeye salmon run in North America. The Fraser salmon are an important part of the province's heritage, and provide a sizable proportion of the total commercial fishing in British Columbia. This power-versus-fish conflict will be faced again if other rivers, such as the Skeena, are viewed as a convenient source of hydro-electric power.

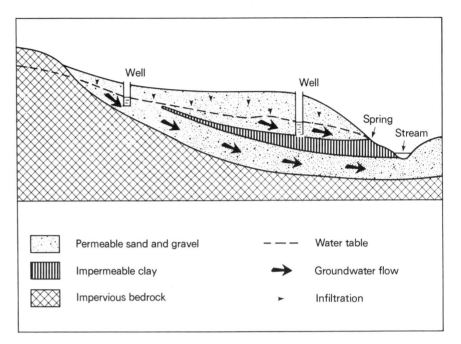

46 Cross-section showing groundwater flow through porous sands and gravels. (Simplified from Geological Survey of Canada, *Geology and Economic Minerals of Canada*, Economic Geology Series No. 1, 1970)

Permeable sand and gravel		— — —	Water table	
Impermeable clay		➡	Groundwater flow	
Impervious bedrock		►	Infiltration	

Groundwater

In the mountains of British Columbia and the Yukon Territory there is generally enough surface water to meet all needs, but in a few areas, industrial, domestic, and agricultural demands are met almost entirely by groundwater. For example, 40 per cent of the water supplied to Lower Mainland communities south of the Fraser River comes from underground sources. Parts of southeast Vancouver Island rely heavily upon groundwater as well.

When water seeps into the ground, it fills cracks in rock, or the pore space in sand and gravel. The upper surface of the zone saturated by groundwater is the water-table: above it, water moves downward. Below the groundwater table, water moves slowly toward springs, streams, lakes or the ocean. Often, the discharging groundwater keeps streams flowing during long periods of dry weather.

A very large quantity of water is stored in the ground, but only part of it is available for use. Any material from which water can be withdrawn for a particular use is called an aquifer (Figure 46). This may be a porous layer of sand or gravel, or a mass of fractured bedrock. The amount of water in an aquifer depends on its porosity (i.e., the open space between grains or the fractures that can hold water). The best underground reservoirs in British Columbia and the Yukon are porous sands and gravels left behind by the retreating ice sheets of the last ice age. A less important source is fractured bedrock. The distribution of groundwater resources is shown in Figure 47.

While the porous materials determine the amount of water that can be stored, it is the climate, especially precipitation, that determines the amount of water available to recharge groundwater aquifers. Aquifers near the surface, which are recharged directly by seepage of rainfall, are *unconfined aquifers*. Deeper *confined aquifers* are fed by water seeping laterally or vertically from aquifers near the surface.

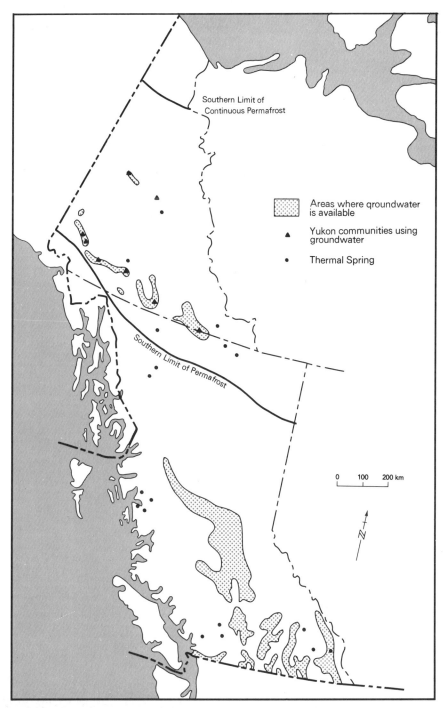

Southern Limit of Continuous Permafrost

Southern Limit of Permafrost

Areas where groundwater is available

▲ Yukon communities using groundwater

• Thermal Spring

0   100   200 km

The amount of water held in unconfined aquifers fluctuates with variations in precipitation, irrigation, drainage, pumping, and land use. In areas where large volumes of groundwater are pumped to the surface during a protracted dry spell, the water table will drop, and wells must be deepened to reach underground reservoirs. Recharge is greatest and groundwater levels are highest during the spring break-up. Levels are lowest in summer, when most of the available moisture is used up by vegetation. The aquifers are recharged in the fall, when precipitation increases and plant growth slows down. Confined aquifers fluctuate much less in their yield of water than unconfined aquifers.

The most heavily used aquifers are the sands and gravels of the lower Fraser Valley. Very little rain falls there in July and August, so nearly all the communities south of the river rely on groundwater for domestic use and irrigation. Towns on the east coast of Vancouver Island (e.g., Duncan, Cowichan) also depend on groundwater supplies, because most of the surface water has been harnessed for hydro-electric power, or pulp and paper production. In the mountainous Interior of British Columbia, surface water meets most of the demands, and large untapped resources of groundwater exist in the glacial deposits on the valley floors, and in porous volcanic rocks.

Groundwater plays a more important role in the Yukon, where rivers and lakes are frozen during the long winter months. In the far north, all the moisture in the soil is solidly frozen to depths up to 450 metres, because average temperatures are below freezing for six or seven months of the year. Summer warmth thaws only the upper layers (from one to four metres), which then turn into a liquid mud. This shallow zone of annual freeze and thaw is called the active layer. The distribution of permafrost in northern British Columbia and the Yukon is shown in Figure 48. Continuous permafrost is found where air temperatures remain below 0°C. Toward the south, continuous permafrost grades into widespread and then scattered permafrost, which is made up of frozen patches separated by areas of unfrozen material. Permafrost restricts the movement of groundwater, so lakes and swamps are common wherever water is unable to drain away from low-lying areas. The development of groundwater supplies in continuous permafrost is either impossible or impractical, especially where the frozen ground extends down to bedrock. However, communities in areas of discontinuous permafrost are able to extract groundwater from unfrozen sands and gravels. Communities along the Alaska Highway get their water supplies from underground sources. Whitehorse uses groundwater to raise the temperature of Yukon River water during cold periods, to prevent freezing and bursting of pipes. The most northerly community to use groundwater is Dawson, where wells have been sunk in nearby Eldorado Creek valley.

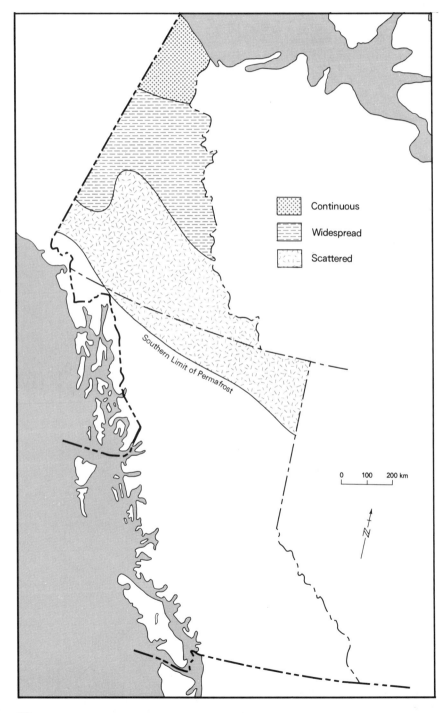

Continuous

Widespread

Scattered

Southern Limit of Permafrost

0   100   200 km

N

Water Quality

Water quality is influenced by natural factors and by the activities of man. The natural quality of water varies from place to place, with the season of the year, and with the kinds of rocks and soils through which it moves. These natural processes which contribute dissolved and suspended material to the water are virtually beyond human control. However, people can control, to varying degrees, the release of industrial, municipal, and agricultural wastes to surface and groundwater supplies.

The word pollution has many meanings. To some people, it means the introduction of pesticides and fertilizers; to others, it means acid mine water or untreated sewage. To the fisherman, pollution may be water temperatures too high for fish to survive. Water quality can be greatly altered by improper use but, even in nature, a lake undergoes slow evolutionary changes from the time of its geological origin to the present. The water of a young lake contains small amounts of dissolved materials essential for plant growth. After many years, dissolved minerals, including plant nutrients such as nitrates and phosphates, increase. The water becomes murky and organic material on the stagnant lake bottom is attacked by bacteria and other decay organisms, producing foul gases.

Man's activities can speed up this natural process of aging. For example, the Okanagan Lake system is faced with a growing influx of sewage and industrial water. Soluble phosphates and nitrates from fertilizers used on the adjacent farm land seep through the ground to the lakes, where they cause algae blooms and dense masses of aquatic weeds. Particularly in the summer months during low flows, the Okanagan River and its tributaries are unable to flush the materials discharged into the lake system, and plant nutrients accumulate rapidly. The dense mats of aquatic plants and algae floating on the lake surfaces are unsightly and interfere with recreational activities such as swimming and boating. In response to all these problems, a federal-provincial study was undertaken between 1969 and 1974 to identify water management options over the next 50 years. As a first step, the two governments intend to co-operate in upgrading waste treatment in the communities bordering Okanagan Lake.

Rivers and streams do have some natural capacity to disperse pollutants discharged into them. However, wastes occur in high concentrations at points of discharge and are also difficult to disperse in constricted reaches or channels, particularly in low-flow periods.

British Columbia and the Yukon Territory are not faced with a major water quality problem yet, but certain local areas are confronted with serious deterioration. This results in damage to commercial and sport fisheries; the closure of recreational beaches because of public health hazard; damage to wildlife habitats, and a general decline in aesthetic quality. A widespread problem is bacterial contamination from untreated domestic sewage discharged into rivers and lakes. Organic waste consumes oxygen as it decays and reduces the amount of oxygen available for freshwater life. At present, dissolved oxygen levels are high in most rivers, except where wastes are released in heavy concentrations into constricted channels and stagnant backwaters. Toxic materials from acid mine wastes, industrial discharge and pesticide residues are found in many of our rivers. Heavy metals such as copper, manganese, and lead do accumulate in the animals of the river-based food chain, but it is not yet clear whether the amounts are large enough to have a serious long-term effect on aquatic life or on the health of people eating fish.

On the whole, groundwater is cleaner than water in rivers and lakes. The soils and rocks through which it percolates screen out many of the harmful bacteria. Groundwater is often more desirable than surface water, because it needs less treatment, and temperature and chemistry are fairly constant. However, its high mineral content in some localities rules out its use for drinking water or irrigation. Septic tank contamination, industrial pollution, and the accumulation of nitrates from agricultural fertilizers will become serious problems, if intensive development continues without sufficient controls over waste discharges. This is particularly the case in valleys such as the lower Fraser and the Okanagan.

3 Land and Forest Resources

The range of latitude (from 49° to 69° N.) and relief of the Cordillera give rise to the greatest climatic diversity in Canada. The cool Mediterranean climate of the Gulf Islands contrasts with the subarctic conditions in northern British Columbia and the Yukon. Tree and plant species are equally varied: sagebrush and cacti grow in the near-desert of the southern Interior, while larch and limber pine endure the harshest of alpine environments.

The landscape is young, having only recently emerged from the last ice age. The soil cover is thin, except where retreating ice-sheets dumped masses of material on the valley floors. Some of the richest soils have developed on alluvial floodplains of the larger rivers, but such fertile areas are very few. Land capable of supporting arable farming covers less than three per cent of the total area, most of it in the south where the climate is favourable to crop production.

The varied relief and geology of the country have a powerful influence upon its climate and soils. In turn, the climate exerts a strong control over the distribution of vegetation and the rate at which soils develop. The history and occurrence of each can be understood in relation to the other features.

Climate

Climate plays a major role in the use of many natural resources: it controls the kinds of crops that can be grown, and the amount of water needed for irrigation. It is equally important for forest operations, from the selection of tree species to fire control. Climate affects stream flows and water storage, and so has a considerable impact on fisheries and flood control. It can be a bane or blessing in the tourist season, and can disrupt transportation links in winter. In the far north and at high altitudes, climate can add to the costs of mining and construction projects.

Air masses which regulate British Columbia's climate originate over the Pacific Ocean and the Arctic. Cold air invades from the northeast, while warmer, moister air moves in over the coast in a series of frontal storms. The coast is dominated by maritime air masses bringing mild, wet winters and cool summers (Figure 49). The prevailing air movement is from the west across the open Pacific, although in winter occasional cold snaps are brought about by outbreaks of arctic air from the northern interior. The Coast Mountains and Cascade Range generally protect the coastal region from invasions of arctic air. They also act as barriers over which Pacific air masses must rise. As the air masses are forced to ascend, they are cooled and lose their moisture in the form of heavy precipitation along the coastal belt. After crossing the mountain barrier, the drier air descends the leeward slopes to produce the Interior dry belt. In the southern part of the Cordillera, eastward moving air masses reach the Columbia and Rocky Mountains, where they are forced to rise again. This produces another rain belt on the west-facing slopes.

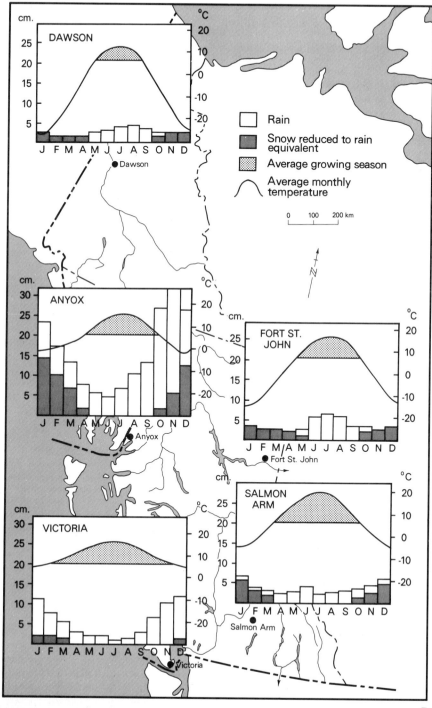

The Interior of British Columbia is the real battleground for maritime and continental air masses. Maritime air penetrating from the coast brings moisture and modifying temperatures. Continental air from the east can bring rapid warming and high summer temperatures, or clear, cold skies in midwinter. Northeastern British Columbia and the Yukon are dominated by arctic air masses which bring extreme winter cold and only moderate summer temperatures (Figure 49). Precipitation is low, because moist, maritime air hardly manages to penetrate the northern Coast Mountains and the St. Elias Range. Thus, the mountain ranges profoundly affect climate by controlling the movement of maritime and continental air masses. Within the mountains, elevation has a major impact on local climate. Precipitation, especially snowfall, increases, and temperatures decrease rapidly with increasing elevation on both west- and east-facing slopes.

Daily and seasonal temperature ranges increase rapidly away from the narrow coastal belt. The moderating influence of the ocean usually penetrates only a few kilometres inland, and nowhere extends beyond 150 kilometres. There is a sharp gradient between the coastal belt and the area east of the Coast Mountains. Average January temperatures hover just above freezing along the coast from Vancouver to Prince Rupert, but fall to well below freezing (-5° to -11°C.) in the B.C. Interior. The Yukon comes under the influence of arctic air masses, and average January temperatures range from -15°C. at Whitehorse to -29°C. at Dawson. Snag, Y.T., holds the North American lowest temperature record for a reading of -63°C.

The growing season is shorter away from the coast and at higher elevations. Southwestern British Columbia, including the lower Fraser valley, has a frost-free period of 180 to 220 days (Figure 50). The modifying effect of maritime air reaches up the Fraser valley as far as Quesnel, where the average frost-free period is 100 to 150 days. Farther north, the growing season shortens rapidly in the face of arctic air masses. Some parts of northern British Columbia and the Yukon have only 50 days without frost each year. East of the Rockies, continental air pushes in to give much of the Peace River district a frost-free period of over 100 days. Along the coast, the onset of frost is often delayed until early December and ends in mid-April. In the Yukon, freezing temperatures are recorded from mid-October through to early May. After this time, it gets warmer until the peak summer months of July and August. In midsummer, mean daily temperatures range from 10° to 18°C. on the coast and increase eastward to between 18°C. and 25°C. in the southern Interior. The summers are hot and dry in the south, but cooler, cloudier and wetter in the north. Very hot days are common in the dry southern valleys, especially the lower Thompson valley, where temperatures are well over 35°C. for many days in succession.

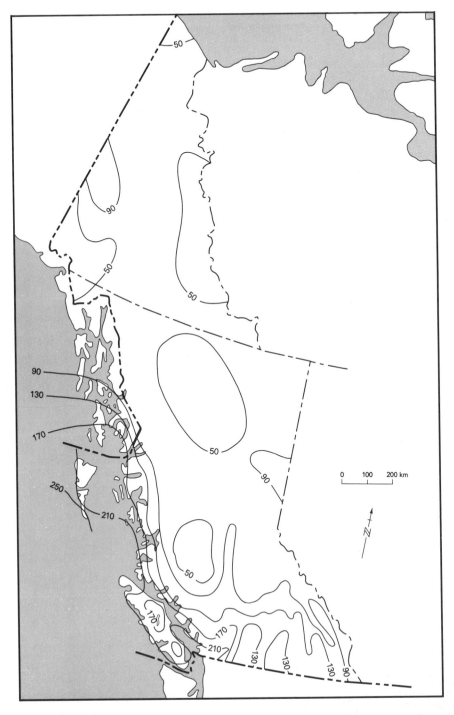

72

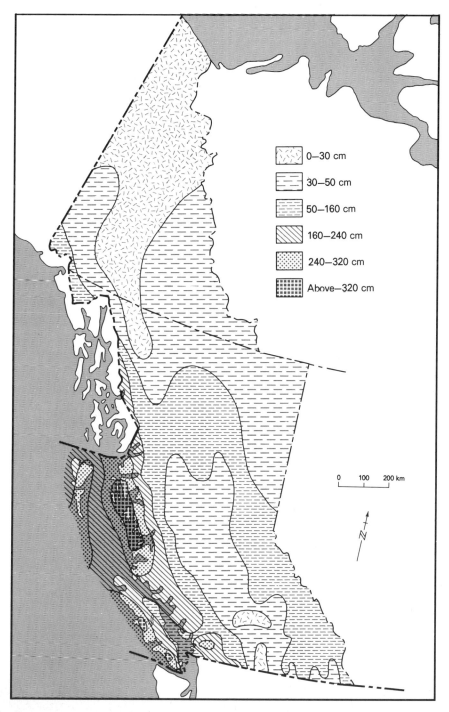

0–30 cm

30–50 cm

50–160 cm

160–240 cm

240–320 cm

Above–320 cm

0 100 200 km

In general, precipitation falls off eastward, especially in the lee of successive mountain ranges (Figure 51). As the air is forced up the western slopes, it loses moisture. As it descends the eastern slopes, it is relatively dry and warm. This orographic effect gives rise to a series of rain belts on west-facing slopes, with rainshadows on the leeward side. The west coast of Vancouver Island receives the full brunt of moist air from the Pacific, and precipitation reaches 400 centimetres on exposed slopes. The Strait of Georgia lies in the rainshadow of the Vancouver Island mountains and receives only 80 to 160 centimetres a year. Air is forced to rise once more over the Coast Mountains, and again the precipitation reaches as much as 400 centimetres. The easterly flowing air becomes steadily drier as it loses moisture on the windward mountain slopes. As a result, some of the southern Interior valleys are truly desert-like, with only 12 to 25 centimetres of precipitation a year. Summer rainfall can be erratic, and prolonged droughts in some years (e.g., 1967 and 1971) lead to extensive outbreaks of forest and brush fires. An eastern rain belt lies over the west-facing slopes of the Columbia and Rocky Mountains, as the eastward flowing airstreams are forced to rise again.

This pattern of rain belts and rainshadows is broken in northern British Columbia, where gaps in the Nass and Skeena Mountains allow maritime air to penetrate into the Interior. Precipitation averages 50 to 80 centimetres a year over much of the region, before falling off to between 40 and 50 centimetres over the Peace River country. The rainshadow effect is extremely strong in the Yukon, where the high St. Elias Range presents a formidable barrier to streams of maritime air. Most of the moisture is lost as snow over the mountains, leaving less than 30 centimetres to fall over the central Yukon each year.

Along the coast, most of the precipitation falls between October and March, when Pacific storms move in from the west. July and August are lowest in rainfall, and irrigation becomes essential for some crops grown in the lower Fraser valley during this period. Storms bring periods of rain to the northern coast, where banks of heavy low cloud still shroud the islands and mainland even in summer. In summer, Prince Rupert has only 110 hours of sunshine per month and a yearly total of 1,035 hours, whereas July and August are the golden months around the southern Strait of Georgia, and Victoria enjoys an average of 2,180 hours of sunshine a year.

In the Interior of British Columbia and the Yukon, precipitation is more evenly distributed throughout the year, although summer tends to be wetter. This trend is most pronounced east of the Rocky Mountains, where wet summers and dry winters follow a pattern also found in the prairies. In the Interior of B.C., winter is the most variable season. The steady eastward progression of Pacific disturbances brings clouds and snow, while arctic air means cold and clear weather.

The far north has two strong seasons. The small amount of sunshine during the short daylight hours of winter causes the land surface to cool. Spring is much later than in the south; as the temperature increases, the snow melts, and ice disappears from the lakes and rivers. There is a rush of plant growth in the long daylight hours of summer. In fact, Whitehorse enjoys almost as many hours of sunshine a year as Vancouver, because the sun hardly dips below the horizon in summer.

Any significant change in the present climate would affect the economy and the environment. For example, a shift to colder and snowier winters would increase heating costs and disrupt transportation links, although ardent skiers would rejoice. Evidence of climatic fluctuations has been collected by botanists studying pollen grains buried in lakes and bogs in order to trace past changes in vegetation (Table 1). From this, scientists know that the Pleistocene ice age, from which the earth is still emerging, began more than one million years ago. A series of glacial advances and retreats left the material from which many of the best soils developed after the ice melted.

Sources: J.C. Ritchie & F.K. Hare,
Quaternary Research 1(1971): 331-342;
R.W. Mathewes & G.E. Rouse, *Canadian Journal of Earth Sciences* 12(1975):
745-756; H.E. Wright & D.G. Frey, *The Quaternary of the United States.*
Princeton University Press, 1965.

Table 1:
Changes in post-glacial Climate and Vegetation

Years Before Present	Vegetation			Climate
	Lower Fraser Valley	Northwest Coast	Northern Yukon	
0	Increasing western hemlock	Sitka spruce, hemlocks	Sedge-tundra	
1,000				Return to cool, moist conditions
			Birch-alder	
2,000				
3,000	Douglas fir and birch important	Alder, Sitka spruce, hemlocks	Spruce	
4,000		Alder at its greatest extent	Alder important	Drier and warmer conditions
5,000				
6,000		Hemlock, Sitka spruce, sedge	Birch-heath, spruce	(growing season 5°C. warmer than now)
7,000	Increase in Douglas fir			
8,000	Western hemlock		Birch, sedge	
9,000	Birch	Willow-birch		
10,000	Decrease in shore and lodgepole pines.	Sedge-heath Tundra	Invasion by spruce, forming forest-tundra Sedge-grass tundra	
11,000	Alder, shore and lodgepole pines			Cold and moist conditions
12,000	Invasion by lodgepole pine	No Record	Willow-birch	
13,000	Willow			

Glacial History

When the climate deteriorated during the last ice age, the glaciers of the St. Elias Range, the Coast Mountains, and the Rockies began to grow and flow into nearby valleys, filling them until only the tallest peaks reared above the ice. At its greatest extent, the ice reached thicknesses up to 2,000 metres in the Interior of British Columbia. Near the sea, where snowfall and ice accumulation was greatest, glaciers escaped through fiords to melt in the open waters of the Pacific Ocean. During the last glacial advance, ice also filled the Strait of Georgia, burying the entire Vancouver area. Approximately 13,000 years ago, the ice began to melt; within a few thousand years, most of the present Interior plateaus and valley country had emerged, covered by a thick mantle of glacial debris.

Strangely enough, the northern and west-central parts of the Yukon were not glaciated during the Ice Age. Apparently, the St. Elias rainshadow did not allow the build-up of glaciers. While plant and animal life was destroyed elsewhere, a few species survived undisturbed in protected areas of the northern Yukon. The placer gold deposits of the Klondike survived primarily because the area escaped the gouging effects of glaciers.

The deposits left behind as the ice receded were the parent material for present soils. Some of them reflect the composition of underlying or nearby rocks, while others include materials carried there from far away. Large lakes dammed up by ice or outwash were drained as the glaciers receded, leaving thick deposits of silt. These silt banks now support rich farmland in the Okanagan and in the Peace River district. The groundwater resources of northern British Columbia and the Yukon are found in the glacial outwash which buried ancient valleys.

As the ice melted, the land surface rebounded from the weight of the glaciers, and streams left banks and terraces along the valley slopes as they cut beds into the loose material. Many such river terraces are now irrigated farmland in the dry southern Interior of British Columbia.

Soils

Climate, vegetation, and drainage all play a part in developing the soil cover. Over ninety per cent of the dry substance of soils is mineral matter, weathered or worn from the original rock. This material is then reworked by the growth and decay of plant life, and by water seeping through from the surface.

Most soils consist of several layers above a more-or-less unchanged original deposit. A layer of undecayed vegetation on the surface merges into an underlying layer of partly decomposed organic material. This gives way to a mixture of organic and mineral matter. These horizons give the soil its quality, depending on texture, mineral content, acidity or alkalinity, and capacity for storing or draining water. Leached and acid soils are called podzols, while soils which have a high mineral content (and hence a high fertility) are called pedocals. Podzols are found under forest cover in moist climates, pedocals under grassland in climates marked by summer drought. Within these two broad families are great variations in soil conditions, depending on elevation, slope, climate, drainage, and vegetation. Elevation is particularly important in mountainous terrain, where tillable soils occur only below 1,250 metres.

52 Cross-section through a grassland (pedocal) soil. The profile consists of two layers, or "horizons." A thick, dark layer rich in humus lies beneath a grass sod. This grades downwards into a lighter-coloured horizon which contains material brought down by water percolating through the upper horizon.
Modified from S.R. Eyre, 1963. *Vegetation and Soils,* London: Edward Arnold.

Metres

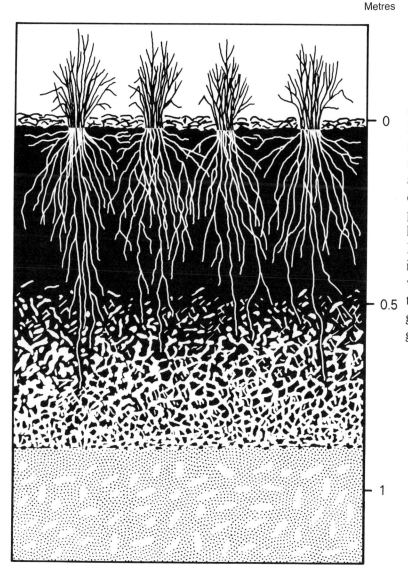

0

0.5

1

Pedocals found in the drier Interior valleys of British Columbia tend to be shallow, with a layer of lime near the surface. Grasses form a dense rooting network throughout this soil, giving it an open, porous texture. Grasses also take up more mineral nutrients than forest species, and thus the humus returned to the soil is much richer. Wind and sun cause evaporation from the soil surface, and a lot of water is lost as the plants transpire. Evaporation and upward movement of water is greater than downward seeping, so the soil nutrients are not leached out; instead, they accumulate and make the soil very fertile. It often consists of a uniform dark-coloured layer which grades into partly weathered parent material (Figure 52). These black soils in the most humid part of the grassland region (around Merritt, Princeton and Kamloops) are the backbone of the ranching industry. If irrigated, they also produce heavy crops of vegetables, alfalfa, and hay. Somewhat similar soils occur in the Bulkley valley, but the best-known are the prairie grassland soils of the Peace River country, which give high grain yields even under difficult climatic conditions.

53 Cross-section through a podzol soil. A layer of leaf mold and acid humus lies on top of the soil surface. Below this there is a thin, acid layer rich in humus followed by a light-coloured, strongly leached horizon. A brownish layer, enriched by material washed down from above, underlies this.
Modified from S.R. Eyre, 1963. *Vegetation and Soils,* London: Edward Arnold.

Podzols are much less fertile, but cover a more extensive area than the grassland soils. They are the result of a wet climate and heavy forest growth. The dense forest cover limits evaporation, so most of the moisture washes down into the ground, leaching out minerals and organic material. This makes the soils acid and of limited agricultural value. There are some differences in the demands of tree species and their impact on the soil. For example, spruce usually grows on heavier, richer soil; in turn, its organic debris contains plenty of mineral nutrients which make the soil less acid. Usually, there is a loose mat of undecayed vegetation over a thin grey layer which has been leached of its organic and mineral content. The break is sharp between decomposed vegetation and the underlying horizon of sand (Figure 53). In the north, the podzol soils are extremely shallow. Peat bogs have developed in areas of poor drainage. Much of the Yukon is under permafrost (Figure 48), and separate soil horizons cannot be distinguished there because of frost heaving, light precipitation, and slow plant growth. As a result, weathering and soil development have not advanced very far.

Some of the most valuable soils of British Columbia are very young. These *alluvial* soils have developed on sand and silt laid down by streams and rivers. They provide some of the richest farmland, but are of very limited extent. The most fertile alluvial soils are in the lower Fraser Valley, the Bella Coola Valley, and the Creston area. However, in some cases the water table lies very near to the surface, so that the land has to be drained and dyked before it can be brought under intensive cultivation. In forested areas, alluvial soils are of value and often support heavy stands of trees.

Organic soils are found in moist areas where plant matter decays rapidly. In some areas, such as the Fraser delta, pockets of organic soil or peat are used for market gardening and berry production.

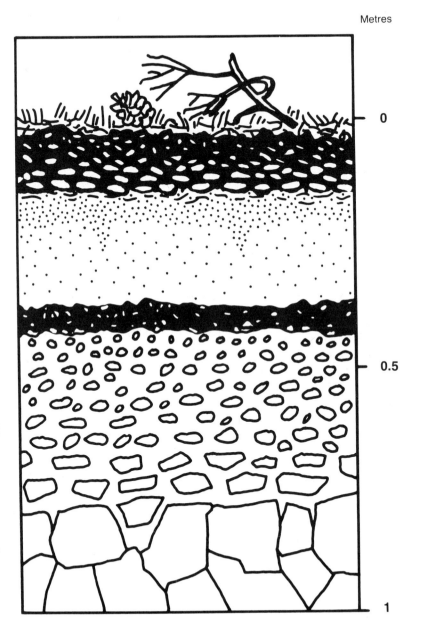

Metres

0

0.5

1

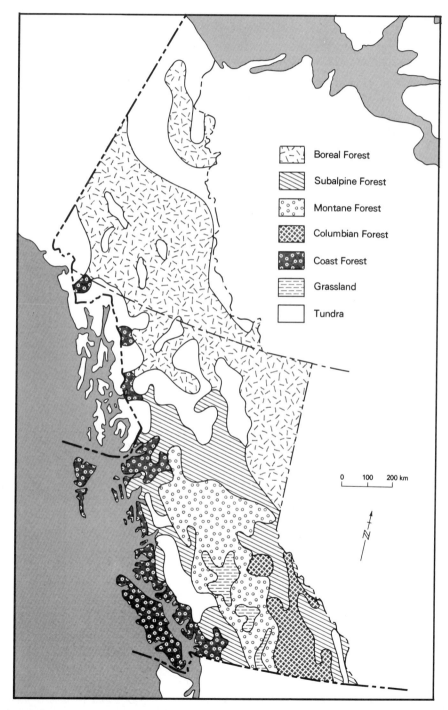

54 The distribution of natural vegetation in British Columbia and Yukon Territory.

Legend:
- Boreal Forest
- Subalpine Forest
- Montane Forest
- Columbian Forest
- Coast Forest
- Grassland
- Tundra

0   100   200 km

Natural Vegetation

If a well drained slope is left completely undisturbed for a long time without human activity, climatic change or other natural disasters, a system of plant communities will establish itself. The plants which grow best under these conditions will dominate to a point at which the vegetation is in balance with the climate and soils: the climatic climax stage. New land is always appearing, and a variety of plant communities succeed each other before a balance is reached with the environment. New mud banks, landslip scars, burnt-over forest, and abandoned farmland are soon invaded by pioneer plants and shrubs that give way to more successful species. Eventually, through this succession, a vegetation emerges which is in balance with the local soil and climate. It is called the natural vegetation of a region.

The natural vegetation of British Columbia and the Yukon matches the diversity of climates, especially precipitation patterns and the range of relief. Within each zone, distinctive communities have evolved: certain species of trees grow together, in company with particular shrubs and flowering plants. Figure 54 shows the distribution of natural vegetation in British Columbia and the Yukon Territory. Vertical contrasts in climate are reflected in distinct vegetation zones on mountain slopes (Figure 55).

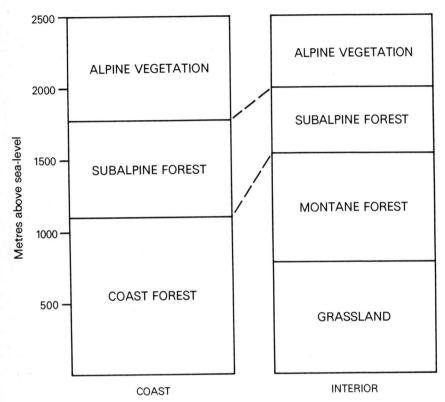

The mild, wet coastal climate has nourished the largest trees known in Canada. Around 1,500 metres above sea level, tree size and density of forest cover decrease as the temperature falls and as soil thins out on the steep, rocky slopes. Above 1,800 metres, the trees give way to alpine meadow and tundra vegetation. Moving eastward into a more arid climate, the forests are more open and the trees smaller, except in the rain belt of the Columbia Mountains. The deep, dry valleys of the southern and central Interior are covered by grassland or semi-desert, grading into open parkland-forest at higher elevations. Farther north, the landscape is dominated by sombre forests (Figure 56). In the Yukon, the upper treeline falls to 1,000 metres or lower, leaving only narrow strips of forest along the valley floors, with tundra vegetation on the slopes above.

The most productive forests grow along the narrow coastal belt. The dominant species of the Coast Forest are western red cedar (*Thuja plicata*) and western hemlock (*Tsuga heterophylla*), along with coast Douglas fir (*Pseudotsuga menziesii*) in the south. Douglas fir is the first conifer to invade cleared areas after fire or logging, because it prefers windy and sunny sites. Given enough time, it is overtopped and crowded out by the moisture-loving cedar and hemlock, except in drier rainshadow areas. The Douglas fir becomes less important as rainfall and exposure increase; north of 50° latitude, it is replaced by Sitka spruce (*Picea sitchensis*). North of the Hecate Strait and on the west coast of Vancouver Island, the western hemlock takes over, with amabilis fir (*Abies amabilis*) on well-drained slopes or western red cedar in moist spots. Dense stands of Sitka spruce grow on alluvial flats along the valley floors and on the coast. Some broadleaved trees are interspersed with conifers in the south, notably red alder (*Alnus rubra*), black cottonwood (*Populus trichocarpa*), and bigleaf maple (*Acer macrophyllum*). Red alder and maple, in particular, are early invaders of areas cleared by logging or fire. Arbutus (*Arbutus menziesii*) and Garry oak (*Quercus garryana*) grow in the southernmost portion, along the southeast coast of Vancouver Island and on the adjacent mainland. This is the

56 The sequence of east-west and
north-south vegetation zones in British
Columbia and Yukon Territory.

most northerly occurrence of the two species, which are found along the Pacific coast in rainshadow areas where the climate is warm and dry.

Moving eastward, the Columbia Forest is very similar to the coastal vegetation, although poorer in species. Western red cedar and western hemlock are the main species of this interior wet belt, which is caused by moist, maritime air streams rising over the Columbia Mountains. Interior Douglas fir (*Pseudotsuga menziesii glauca*) also grows in this zone; it has adapted to the climate, which is a little drier than along the coast.

The Montane Forest is the result of the arid climate of the central Interior. Because the climate is dry, soil texture, aspect, and exposure have a subtle influence on the distribution of tree species in this zone. South of 51° N., Ponderosa pine (*Pinus ponderosa*) and interior Douglas fir grow in open parkland country with bunch-grass prairie and weeds, depending on the grazing history. On steep slopes above 1,100 metres, interior Douglas fir forest takes over, with stands of trembling aspen (*Populus tremuloides*) and lodgepole pine (*Pinus contorta*). Farther north, Engelmann spruce (*Picea engelmanii*) and alpine fir (*Abies lasiocarpa*) intrude from the subalpine forest on the higher slopes, and western white birch (*Betula papyrifera*) comes in. Towards the northern limit of the Montane Forest, before the transition into Boreal Forest, white spruce (*Picea glauca*) becomes an important commercial species.

Grassland vegetation covers the lower valleys and adjacent slopes of the northern and central Interior. Although grassland catches the eye of travellers through the dry valleys of southern British Columbia, the total area is not large. Between 900 and 1,200 metres, it gives way to the open parkland of the Montane Forest. The vegetation of the grassland is very sensitive to small changes in climate and human use. Under natural conditions, there are often three zones of grassland, each with different soils and mix of species. Sagebrush (*Artemisia* species) and other semi-desert shrubs are common on the lower slopes, while perennial bunch-grasses provide increasing cover at higher elevations.

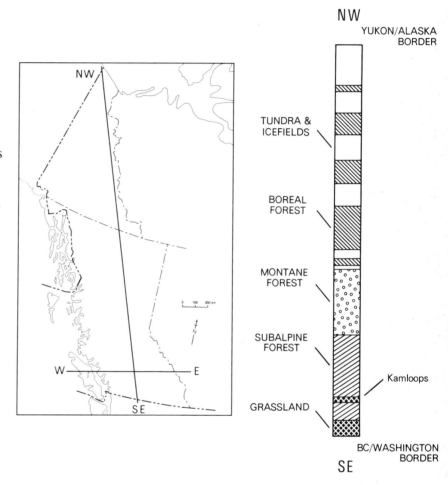

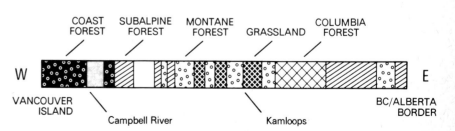

Sagebrush has become more widespread since large-scale settlement began in the late 1850s. Soon after this time, most of the grasslands were being grazed, and the lower slopes were exhausted because of overstocking. As a result, only a small proportion of the region still has its natural climax vegetation of bunch-grass. Sagebrush has taken over because of overgrazing.

Subalpine Forest occupies the high mountain slopes in the Interior and along the coast. The major species are Engelmann spruce, lodgepole pine, and alpine fir. Along the coast, it appears on slopes above the Coastal Forest around 1,000 metres, where mixed coniferous stands of amabilis fir, mountain hemlock (*Tsuga mertensiana*), and alpine fir extend up to the treeline. In northern British Columbia, it is the principal forest zone of the Interior. Toward its northern margins, more and more species such as the black and white spruce (*Picea mariana* and *P. Glauca*) intrude from the Boreal Forest. With increasingly tougher climate and soil conditions, the Boreal Forest gives way to an open lichen-woodland which merges into tundra. A sombre landscape of black and white spruce, jack pine (*Pinus banksiana*) and alpine fir is sporadically brightened by white birch and trembling aspen.

The best forests in the central Yukon are on the protected lowlands, but tree growth deteriorates quickly with elevation. The mountain slopes are covered by an open parkland of white spruce, willow (Salix) and trembling aspen, up to a treeline at 1,000 to 1,500 metres. Farther north, near Dawson, stunted stands of white and black spruce change to dwarf birch (*Betula glandulosa*) and alpine tundra at 1,000 metres above sea level.

A varied patchwork of plant communities survives on the tundra of the north and at high elevations in the south. Shrub and heath are commonly found on sheltered slopes, particularly where the soil thaws in summer. Arctic heath, alpine bearberry (*Arctostaphylos alpina*), and Labrador tea (*Ledum glandulosum*) form a low scrub, separated by patches of dwarf willow and birch. Farther north, in the continuous permafrost zone, the ground is only half-covered by lichens, sedges, grasses and small flowering plants. Winter winds, severe frost, a short growing season, and permafrost make it impossible for trees to survive. Spring flowers emerge through melting snowdrifts, and masses of flowers carpet the alpine meadows during the summer months. The plants growing on the highest slopes in southern British Columbia must be able to survive frequent droughts caused by the intensive light, extreme temperatures, and strong winds. Similarly, the vegetation of the arctic tundra must survive winter droughts caused by very low temperatures and strong winds.

The Forest Resource

Wood was very important in the material culture of the Northwest Coast Indians. They used cedar for their houses, totem poles, and seagoing canoes. They carved utensils from cedar, hemlock, spruce, and other species, and wove hats and cloaks from bark fibre. Although wood was an integral part of native life, their use of forest materials was negligible by modern standards. From modest beginnings in the mid-nineteenth century, the forest industry has grown to be a mainstay of the B.C. economy. It plays only a very small role in the Yukon.

In the early days of land clearance, forests were considered a nuisance. The market for timber developed as settlements grew larger and as export trade was established. The logging and sawmilling industry grew up along the southern coast in the 1850s, moved northward and eventually expanded into the Interior. At present, British Columbia supplies most of the sawn lumber and plywood, and one quarter of the chemical pulp produced in Canada. The province's forest land supports half of the saw timber volume remaining in Canada.

Almost sixty per cent of British Columbia and the Yukon is forested, but not all of this land supports mature stands of commercial value. Commercial timber covers one third of B.C., but only one-tenth of the Yukon Territory. The remaining forest consists of immature stands, species of no commercial value, or sites with poor growing conditions. Fifteen species, mostly coniferous, are useful for a wide variety of wood products. Western hemlock, Douglas fir, the spruces, and true firs (Abies ssp.) are the main species used for sawn lumber. Cedar, Douglas fir, and hemlock are suited for pulp production.

The coast was the cradle of the forest industry in British Columbia and still contains most of the remaining mature stands of western hemlock, cedar, Douglas fir, and Sitka spruce. The heaviest stands in the more accessible areas were soon logged. Western hemlock comprises 40 per cent of the total volume of timber.

Different species and smaller trees are found in the Interior, where the climate does not promote such rapid growth as on the coast. Spruce dominates, but lodgepole pine, interior Douglas fir, and the true firs are important. The range of species decreases northward as the growing season shortens and the climate becomes more severe. In the Prince George area and north of latitude 56°, the spruce and true firs of the Boreal Forest are the most important commercial species. The only valuable timber in the Yukon occurs in the south, along the major river valleys: 60 per cent of the Yukon's forest cover grows in the Liard basin near the B.C. border.

The productivity of forests decreases northward and is limited to low elevations, because the physical environment restricts tree growth. Commercial timber, for example, is usually found 300 metres or more below the treeline. Most trees mature in 70 to 120 years, although stands at higher latitudes or higher altitudes may take as long as 200 years. Douglas fir or western hemlock on a good coastal site will mature in 80 years, compared to 140 to 160 years for Interior white pine. Individual trees in the Coast Forest also reach a greater size. On good sites, stands can be three times more productive than those in the Interior, although there are variations depending on species and soil conditions.

The History of Logging, Sawmilling and Manufacturing

Commercial logging began in British Columbia during the 1840s on Vancouver Island. There was little market for lumber until the 1850s, when external trade began. The early logging sites were close to tidewater along the southern coast of Vancouver Island. The trees were felled by axe, pulled down to the shore, and floated to nearby sawmills which used fast-running streams as their source of power.

As the more accessible stands were cut, logging operations moved north along the east coast of Vancouver Island. The gold discoveries along the Fraser River and in the Cariboo created a demand for lumber on the mainland of B.C. However, primitive technology still kept logging sites close to the mills. Manpower and gravity-hauling gave way to teams of oxen and horses which dragged logs to the water's edge, thus expanding the range of log transportation to three or four kilometres. The sawmills were often temporary and were moved every few years, once the accessible timber had been felled.

Logging operations in the Yukon have largely depended on the state of the mining industry. There was a tremendous demand for lumber during the Klondike gold rush. When the population of Dawson City reached 20,000 in the summer of 1897, 12 sawmills produced construction timber for the townsite and lumber for flumes and sluice boxes. Large quantities of wood were also used for heating and as fuel for the stern-wheelers plying the Yukon River.

Much of the good timber near Dawson City had been cut by 1930, and the sawmill industry of the Yukon virtually disappeared. After that, most of the lumber was imported from British Columbia until World War II, when large volumes were cut during the construction of the Alaska Highway. Logging then expanded slowly in the Liard area to supply fuel wood and mining timber, but substantial amounts are imported from B.C. to meet the local demand. The Yukon sawmilling industry has been restricted by the quality of timber, limited access to the forested land, and high operating costs. At present, ten small sawmills in the Watson Lake area tap the forest resources of the Liard basin. Their total capacity is less than one per cent of British Columbia's production.

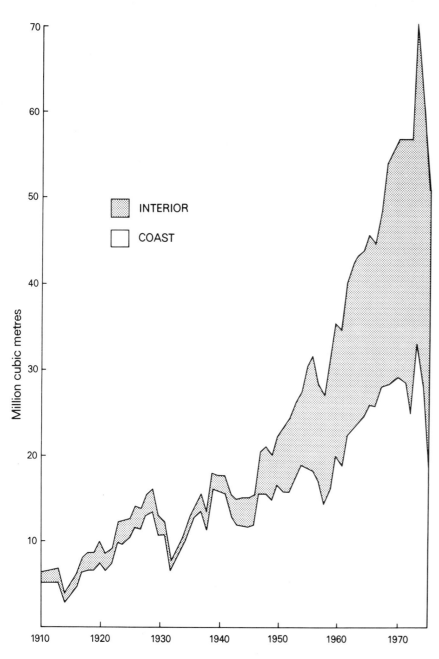

57 The volume of timber logged in British Columbia, 1910-1975. (Sources: *Inventory of the Natural Resources of British Columbia,* 1964 and B.C. Forest Service, annual reports)

In British Columbia, the giant trees along the coast were selectively logged, because of the amount of effort required to fell and transport them. This practice of high-grading was extremely wasteful, and many smaller trees were damaged or left on the ground.

The arrival of the Canadian Pacific Railway at Vancouver in 1886 forged new trade connections, and lumber exports to the United States and Europe increased rapidly. At the turn of the century, steam power replaced animal power and gravity-hauling. As the technology improved and the more accessible stands were cut, logging penetrated inland.

The expansion of the railroads opened up the forested valleys of the Interior, although most of the logging was still concentrated in southwestern British Columbia. The construction of logging railways allowed logging camps to be set up some distance away from the milling sites. With mechanization, companies switched to clear-cutting along the railway lines, but only the larger trees were taken out. Small trees and debris were left behind.

Improvements in felling methods allowed production to increase rapidly. The introduction of chain saws and hydraulic lift systems gave an enormous boost to the scale of logging operations after the Depression (Figure 57). Although tractors and trucks had appeared before World War I, their major impact was not felt until after 1945. From the 1950s onward, major growth shifted to the Interior, as road construction opened up previously inaccessible forest land. Many portable mills were constructed along the new transportation routes, and these were moved as the local forests were depleted. Eventually, they gave way to a smaller number of stationary mills with a higher capacity, using logs hauled by truck from a large tributary area.

58 The distribution of sawmills in British Columbia and Yukon Territory.

Source: B.C. Forest Service, 1973. *The British Columbia Forest Industry: Its Direct and Indirect Impact on the Economy.*

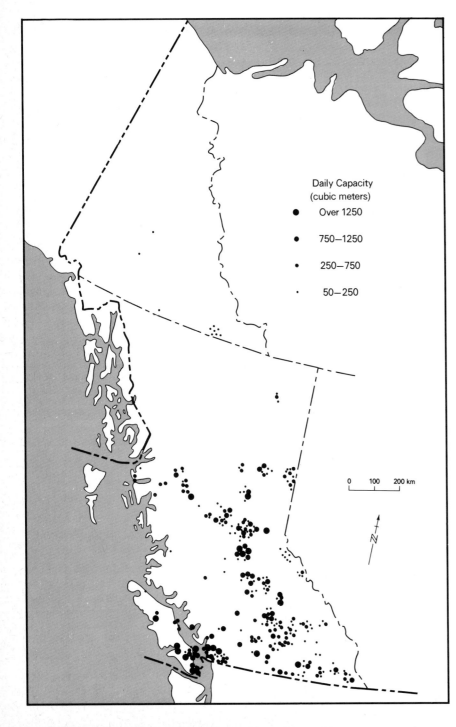

Daily Capacity
(cubic meters)

● Over 1250

● 750—1250

• 250—750

· 50—250

0   100   200 km

Although the Interior forest industry now equals the coast in lumber production (Table 2), the large integrated pulp and sawmills are concentrated in the traditional core area of southwestern British Columbia (Figures 58 and 59). Some of these coastal sawmills use wood transported from as far away as Prince Rupert and the Queen Charlotte Islands.

The total volume of timber harvested increased threefold between 1950 and 1970, but there has been a major decline in the last few years, largely because of a slump in the lumber market of the United States. The postwar housing boom in North America has slackened off, and the demand for construction timber has fallen. Immediately after World War II, three-quarters of the total cut continued to be taken from the Coast Forest. At present, well over half comes from the Interior. The distribution of the commercial species harvested in British Columbia and the Yukon is shown in Figure 60.

Table 2:
The Distribution of Forest Product Industries in British Columbia, 1970

	Lumber (per cent)	Plywood (per cent)	Pulp (per cent)
Coast	49	78	79
Southern Interior	25	13	9
Northern Interior	26	9	12

59 The distribution of pulp and paper mills in British Columbia.

60 Principal species logged in the forest administrative districts of British Columbia and Yukon Territory.

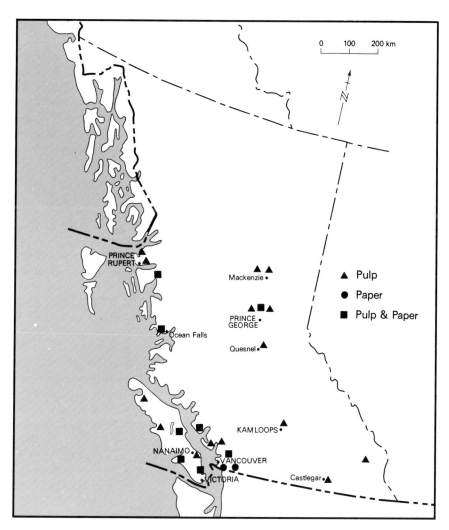

Pulp
Paper
Pulp & Paper

Mackenzie
PRINCE RUPERT
PRINCE GEORGE
Ocean Falls
Quesnel
KAMLOOPS
NANAIMO
VANCOUVER
VICTORIA
Castlegar

0 100 200 km

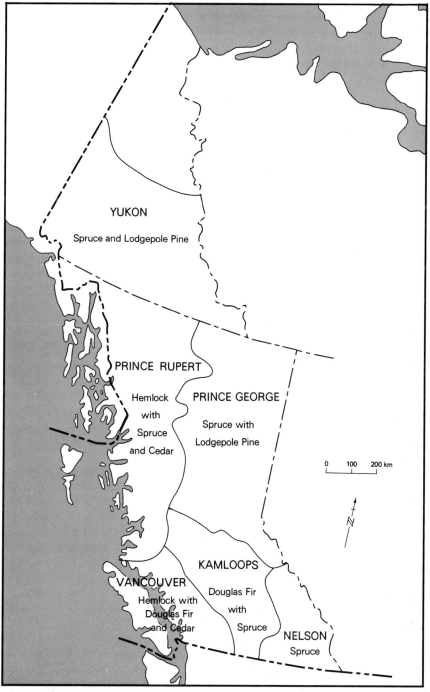

YUKON
Spruce and Lodgepole Pine

PRINCE RUPERT
Hemlock with Spruce and Cedar

PRINCE GEORGE
Spruce with Lodgepole Pine

VANCOUVER
Hemlock with Douglas Fir and Cedar

KAMLOOPS
Douglas Fir with Spruce

NELSON
Spruce

0 100 200 km

Source: B.C. Forest Service, annual reports.

Western red cedar and the hemlock species make up one third of the annual cut in British Columbia, followed by Douglas fir, spruce, the true firs, and lodgepole pine (Table 3). Douglas fir has been logged intensively, particularly on the coast. At present, this species represents only 7 per cent of the total mature timber volume, but makes up 18 per cent of the annual cut. Fifteen years ago, as much as one third of the timber harvested was Douglas fir. For sawn lumber and pulp, other species are being substituted, and the annual cut of both hemlock and spruce now exceeds the Douglas fir harvest.

Approximately three quarters of the B.C. log harvest is now converted into sawn lumber. Fifteen per cent is used in pulp production, and the remaining ten per cent is converted into plywood, shingles, and other minor products. Most of these industries are concentrated in the coastal region (Table 2).

Table 3:
British Columbia: The Mature Forest Resource and Its Use

Species	Volume Available (per cent)	Volume Cut (per cent)
Hemlock (mainly *Tsuga heterophylla*)	22	22
Spruces (*Picea* spp.)	24	22
True Firs (*Abies* spp.)	18	13
Lodgepole pine (*Pinus contorta*)	13	10
Western red cedar (*Tsuya plicata*)	11	13
Douglas fir (*Pseudotsuga menziesii*)	7	18
Other species	5	2

The Management of Forest Resources

Most of the forest resources of British Columbia and the Yukon are owned by the public. In B.C., the decision to retain Crown ownership was made in 1865, and only four per cent of the forest land was sold or given away as Crown Grants during the nineteenth century. This legacy of public control has made it easier to introduce a sustained yield programme designed to manage the forest as a renewable resource.

The British Columbia government adopted the policy of sustained yield forestry in 1953, to ensure a continuing timber supply. Under this policy, two types of forest holdings were created. The *Tree Farm Licence* was designed to encourage careful management of the forests by leasing public land to established companies for a 21-year (renewable) period. The terms of the lease include sustained yield practices, disease control, and fire protection. Within *Public Sustained Yield Units*, the provincial government maintains direct control, but auctions the cutting rights to logging companies. Most of the Tree Farm Licences are in the Coast Forest, while the Public Sustained Yield Units are concentrated in the Interior.

To ensure a perpetual timber supply from the forests, the annual harvest must not exceed the annual growth. After making allowances for all the losses caused by insects, diseases, fire and wind, the annual allowable cut is calculated by estimating the net volume of mature timber (i.e., after losses), its annual growth, and the rotation age.

The period needed for a species to reach maturity is its rotation age. Many foresters consider that trees should be cut down once they have reached maturity, because less wood is added each year as they grow older. For example, a western hemlock growing on a good coastal site may produce 30 cubic metres of usable wood in its first 80 years, but after that the growth rate slows down, and the toll from insects and disease rises.

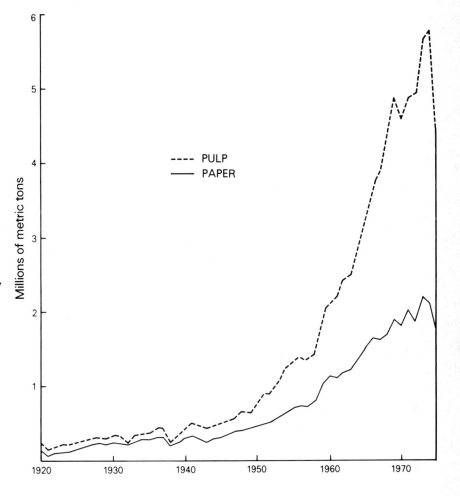

61 Pulp and paper production in British Columbia, 1920-1975. (Sources: *Inventory of the Natural Resources of British Columbia,* 1964 and B.C. Dept. of Industrial Development, Trade and Commerce, *Summary of Economic Activity,* annual)

The slow growth rate and long rotations of tree species in the northern forests increase the size of the forest area needed to supply a sawmill perpetually. Whereas two crops could be harvested in 180 years from a coastal stand, only one crop could be harvested in the same time-span in northern British Columbia or the Yukon. Because of longer rotation periods, the northern sawmills depend on larger areas of forest for a permanent supply of timber. The total volume of timber logged on the coast each year is very close to the allowable cut, but there is considerable potential for expansion in the Interior, particularly within the northern forests where the present cut is below established limits.

The sustained yield policy has placed attention on careful forest management. In the early days, only the best parts of trees were used: tall stumps and small-diameter trunks were left behind. Such wasteful practices are rapidly disappearing, because small trees or waste can now be fed into pulp mills as wood chips.

The pulp and paper industry of B.C. began around 1910, but progress was slow until old mills expanded and new ones were built after 1945. The increasing demand for pulp and paper between 1950 and 1965 led to the construction of eight new mills, including the first in the Interior. More mills have been added since then, and the pulp and paper industry now plays a major role in British Columbia's economy. The pre-war industry focussed on newsprint and sulphite pulp, which was exported to the United States. It expanded after 1945, because of a growing demand for sulphite pulp to feed the chemical industries making rayon, cellophane, and other products. Most of the demand, however, has been for sulphate pulp for cartons and packaging materials. Paper manufacturing has grown much more slowly, and a great quantity of the pulp is still exported without conversion into paper products. Production has fluctuated widely since the late 1960s, and has declined greatly in the last few years, because of an oversupply in the export pulp and newsprint markets (Figure 61).

In 1972, the B.C. provincial government introduced guidelines to improve coastal logging practices which had previously damaged the forest environment. Extensive clear-cutting and logging road construction had led to soil erosion; on steep slopes, silt and log debris washed into valuable spawning streams, and commercial trees did not grow back on large logged areas. Clear-cutting is now limited to a maximum area of 80 hectares, and stands must be left between the cut-over areas. The guidelines also call for better preparation of the logging sites before they are restocked with seedlings.

Until about forty years ago, government and industry relied on natural regeneration to restock logged or burned forest land. Reforestation on a small scale began before World War II. Since then, seed collection and seedling production have accelerated (Figure 62). Replanting began in the Interior during the mid 1950s, expanded rapidly in the late 1960s, and now equals the coast effort. However, the cut still exceeds the replanting programme.

62 The total area of British Columbia replanted each year with coniferous seedlings, 1945-1975. (Source: B.C. Forest Service, annual reports). Survival of the seedlings depends on climate, animal damage, insects, disease, competition from other species, and the care taken during site preparation.

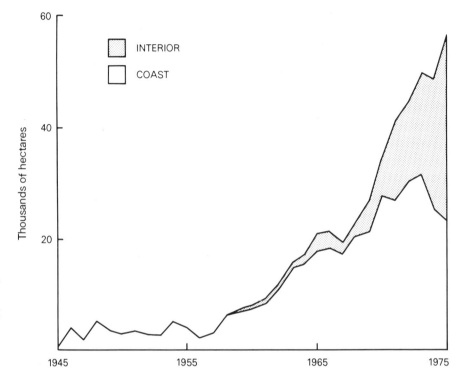

Improved strains of trees have been developed by selecting the best trees and using them as parents in the seedling nurseries. Seeds and small branches taken from these superior *plus* trees are used to produce seedlings and cuttings. Douglas fir has been the most popular species for reforestation, particularly on the coast where it grows rapidly and produces tall, straight timber. Spruce, lodgepole pine and other species have been used to a smaller extent (Figure 63). Subalpine species have proved more difficult to grow in nurseries or restocked areas. The long-term effect of concentrating on a few major species will reduce the variety found in coastal and southern Interior forests. The smaller range of species will make the forests more vulnerable to new diseases or insect invasions.

Forests are no longer regarded solely as a source of commercial timber: the same land is used to support fish and wildlife populations, domestic livestock, and recreational activities. Conflicts have developed between some of these land uses, and more care must be taken to balance logging and other activities.

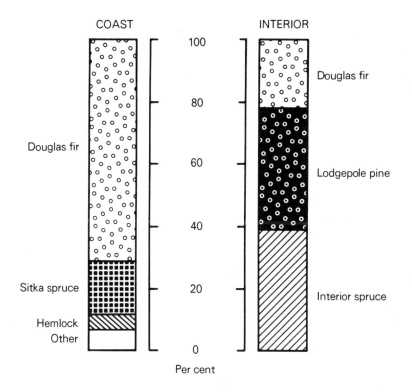

64 The distribution of principal farming
regions in British Columbia and Yukon
Territory.

Agriculture

Land suitable for farming in the Canadian Cordillera is restricted to the valley bottoms, the low intermontane basins and the plains of northeastern British Columbia. Less than two per cent of the land surface can be used for cultivation, and only half of this area has been improved for arable farming. The soils and climate have led to regional specialization in the types of agriculture. The north is climatically unsuitable for intensive cultivation because of summer frosts. Large areas in the south are covered by leached and acidic soils; in many regions, the low-lying land is badly drained or the climate is too dry for farming.

One third of the improved land in British Columbia lies in the coastal valleys and on the eastern lowlands of Vancouver Island. The extremely fertile floodplain of the lower Fraser River dominates this region. The Interior valleys, particularly the Okanagan basin, form another major pocket containing 40 per cent of the improved land in the province. The remaining cultivated land is found in the Peace River plain, with a smaller pocket in the Nechako pioneer farming belt west of Prince George (Figure 64). Most of the unimproved land in the valleys and intermontane basins of the Cariboo-Chilcotin region is used for grazing. In the Yukon, the short growing season, the limited area of fertile soils, and widespread permafrost has severely restricted the development of agriculture; potential farmland is confined to the southern valleys around Whitehorse and Carcross.

Spasmodic attempts were made at farming during the fur-trading days, but the agricultural industry in British Columbia did not get underway until the gold rushes created a demand for farm products. Agriculture began on southern Vancouver Island, but it was hampered by the cost of clearing and draining the heavily forested land and by the small size of the local market. Within a few years, the farmers also faced competition from cereal grains grown in California and Oregon.

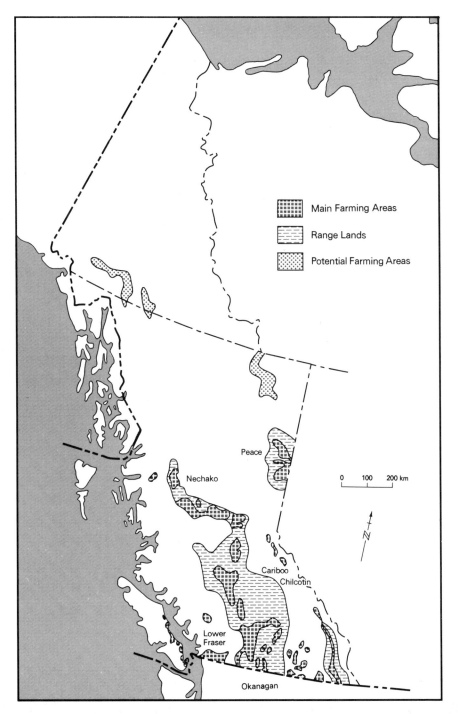

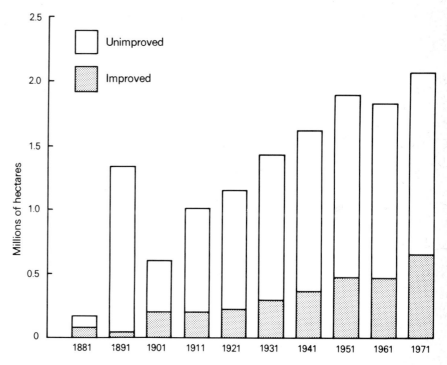

65 The total area of improved and unimproved farmland in British Columbia, 1881-1971. (Sources: M.C. Urquhart and H.A.H. Buckley, eds. *Historical Statistics of Canada*, 1965 and Canada Year Book, annual)

Agriculture prospered during the Fraser and Cariboo gold rushes. By 1865, cattle ranches were established along the Thompson valley west of Kamloops. Some cattle were driven across the United States border to supply beef to the mining towns, but within a few years large-scale cattle ranching had developed in the Okanagan and Nicola valleys.

From the beginning, the farmers were handicapped by the difficulty of transporting produce over long distances through difficult country. The construction of wagon roads helped the cattle industry to flourish in the Okanagan valley during the 1880s and 1890s. The completion of the transcontinental railway in 1886 stimulated ranching and farming, because it attracted people and industry to the province (Figure 65). It seemed that a market had opened up with the east-west link to the prairie provinces, but B.C. farmers found, instead, that it created competition on their home market. In many areas of B.C., the production costs were higher than in Alberta; the local wheat farmers, in particular, could not meet the competition.

At the turn of the century, large-scale ranching continued in the Cariboo-Chilcotin district but, in other areas, farming became more specialized. Dairy farming was concentrated in the lower Fraser valley, and fruit crops were being grown in the Okanagan by 1908.

As late as 1905, British Columbia was importing more farm produce than it was exporting. Within a decade, the local farms could meet the local demand, but farmers still complained about competition from the prairies and American farmers. The expense of clearing the land, supplying irrigation water, or draining the valley bottoms made production costs very high. Machinery had to be imported from the east, and there were still the problems of transportation. In the end, the greatest inhibition was the high cost of improving the remaining farmlands.

The last large agricultural area to be developed was the Peace River country, which was opened up in the 1920s. Rail transportation linked the northern prairie of Alberta to the major eastern markets, and land development spilled over into the plains of northeastern British Columbia. During the same period, new rail links encouraged agricultural pioneers to settle in the Bulkley and Nechako valleys west of Prince George.

Farming in the Yukon will probably never be as important as it was during the Klondike gold rush, when small farms produced potatoes and other garden vegetables, milk, beef, hay and other crops. By 1931, only forty farms remained, and many of these have since been abandoned. There was a temporary revival in the 1950s and early '60s when farming was encouraged, but by 1966 another decline had set in and only nine farms were left. Most field crops cannot ripen during the short growing season, and many are damaged by summer frosts. The cost of raising livestock is excessive, because open grazing is limited and long indoor wintering is essential. Native grasses are widespread, but they do not grow abundantly. Garden crops can be grown, but their yields are uncertain. Equipment and supplies are more expensive because of the high transportation costs. Thus, the Yukon imports most of its food by road and rail.

In British Columbia, the drift of people away from rural areas to the towns began before World War II. In 1931, 15 per cent of the population lived on farms; forty years later, this had fallen to three per cent. The number of farms has declined, and the remaining operations have consolidated into larger, more capital-intensive units which employ less labour. The one exception to this general pattern is the small-holding. The small farm scene has not changed very much over the last 50 years; still one quarter of all the operations are less than four hectares.

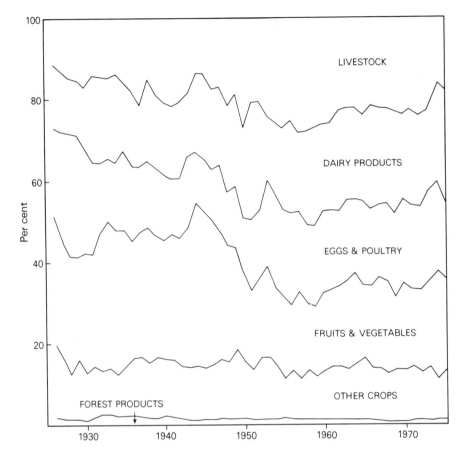

66 The relative contributions of crops and livestock to the value of agricultural production in British Columbia, 1920-1975. (Sources: Statistics Canada Catalogues 21-201, 21-511 and *Canada Year Book,* annual)

High capital and operating costs make farming expensive in British Columbia, and farmers continue to face competition from imported produce. Good agricultural land is very limited, and some of the best areas have been invaded by urban sprawl. By 1972, erosion of the province's farmland by urban land uses had reached 5,700 hectares a year. Most of this was in highly productive areas: the lower Fraser valley and the Okanagan valley.

In 1973, the B.C. provincial government passed legislation to preserve agricultural lands for farm use, and much of the richest farm land is now protected in agricultural reserves. Farming still faces problems, but it is now possible to maintain a viable agricultural economy (Figure 66). If more fertile valley land had disappeared under asphalt and concrete, British Columbia would have been forced to rely even more heavily on agricultural imports.

The Coastal Valleys

The lower Fraser valley and the east coast lowlands of Vancouver Island contain the most valuable farmlands in British Columbia. The Fraser valley alone produces more than half the total value of agricultural products in the province. A combination of physical advantages and historical development have made this the most highly developed farming region in B.C.

The first large farm was cleared by the Hudson's Bay Company in 1827, and more extensive lowland areas on the delta were converted to farmland in the 1860s. The construction of the Canadian Pacific Railway through the valley created a growing market which stimulated more land clearance.

The floodplain of the Fraser River is covered by alluvial soils, which are very valuable because of their fine texture and rich organic content (Figure 67). Much of the land is less than 15 metres above sea level. Therefore, poor natural drainage and frequent flooding demands heavy investment in drainage and dyking. Glacial soils form rolling uplands between 100 and 300 metres above sea level, but these areas are not as fertile as the alluvial soils.

The moist, moderate climate has encouraged specialized farming. Winter pasturing of cattle is possible because the average temperatures are above freezing in winter, so dairy products for the Vancouver market are the basis of the agricultural industry. Forage crops and pasture that support the dairy herds cover most of the arable land. Poultry and egg production are also favoured by the closeness of a large urban market. Together, dairy produce and poultry contribute three quarters of the value of agricultural products in the valley.

The climate also supports production of vegetables, small fruits, and horticultural crops such as flowers and ornamental shrubs. The vegetables and small fruits (strawberries, blueberries, cranberries, etc.) are grown mainly on the rich lowland soils. Orchard fruits are cultivated on the upland areas.

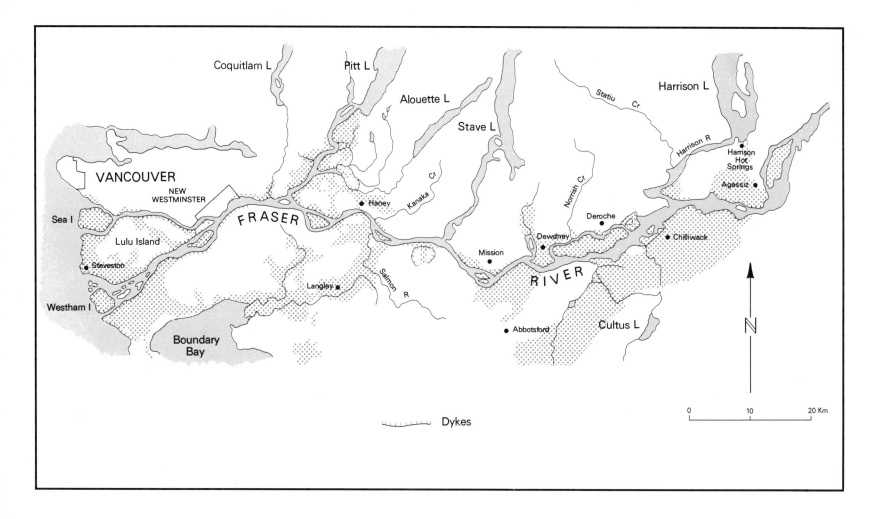

Pockets of farmland are found on the post-glacial deltas and drained lake-bottoms of the east coast lowlands on Vancouver Island. There are scattered patches of alluvial soil, but most of the soils are leached and fertilizers must be applied to improve the yield. Dairy and poultry farming, together with the cultivation of vegetables and soft fruits, are important. Spring flowers are grown for the central and eastern Canadian markets, taking advantage of the early spring season in the Victoria region.

Other small areas of improved farmland are widely scattered on narrow coastal plains, on deltas at the heads of fiords, and in the small intermontane basins of the Coast Range. The cool, moist climate and the leached, acidic soils are only able to support subsistence farms. Many of them are worked on a part-time basis, and farm income has to be supplemented by fishing or logging. Farms near Bella Coola, Terrace, Pemberton Meadows, and on the Queen Charlotte Islands support cattle and root crops such as potatoes.

The Southern Interior Valleys

The Okanagan valley is the outstanding farming area in the Interior, contributing 20 per cent of the total agricultural production of B.C. Arable land is confined to the floor and low terraces of the narrow, deep-sided valley. Because the rainfall is less than 30 centimetres a year, the availability of irrigation water was an important factor in the development of agriculture (Figure 68).

Soils and vegetation reflect the climatic diversity of the valley. Deep soils on the valley floor and rich silt deposits on the terraces give way to podzols on the higher slopes. However, summer temperatures in the valley are high, and the water shortage can only be overcome by drawing irrigation water from the lakes in the Okanagan valley. Another climatic drawback is spring frost, which is particularly harmful to the fruit trees.

In the late nineteenth century, land companies bought large cattle ranches, installed irrigation systems and planted fruit trees. Fruit production began when the land was subdivided and sold as small-holdings. The speculative fruit boom collapsed before World War I, because of the high cost of irrigation and transportation. In addition, a series of killing frosts helped to weaken the industry.

Improvements came slowly in the 1920s, when co-operative marketing schemes were set up to combat the problem of distant markets and competition. Presently, the valley is dominated by fruit trees, market gardening, and dairying. Fruit is the only major export crop produced in British Columbia.

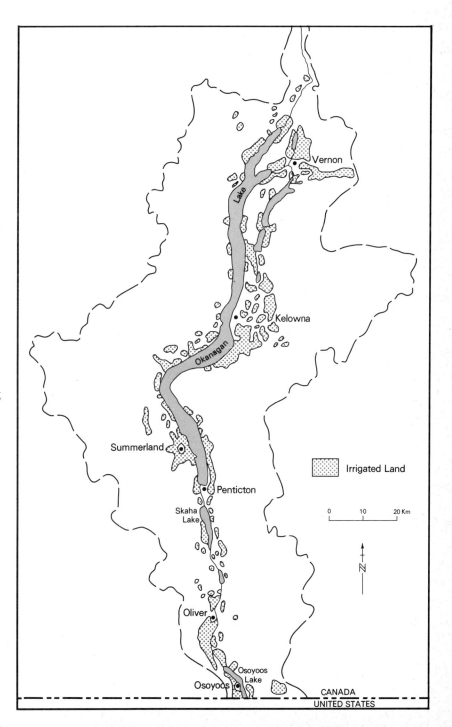

97

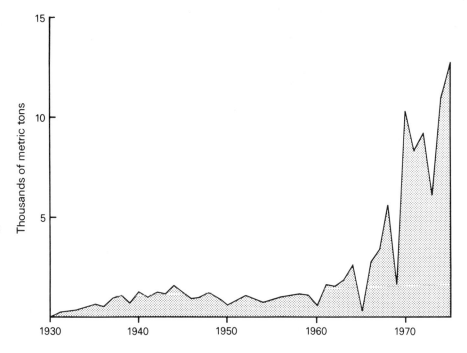

69 Grape production in British Columbia, 1930-1975. (Source: Statistics Canada Catalogues 22-003 and 21-512)

The climate in the Okanagan favours the cultivation of tender stone fruits. Peaches, apricots, and grapes are concentrated in the southern Okanagan, where the growing season lasts over 215 days. The orchards are on the terraces and lower slopes, where circulating air protects them from late spring and early fall frosts. Specialized fruits and vegetables, including tomatoes and cucumbers, ripen by midsummer. The most rapidly expanding crop in the Okanagan is the grape (Figure 69). Hybrid varieties from European and North American grape stocks have been used to improve the production of B.C. wines.

Some winter wheat is grown on the higher slopes, which are also devoted to livestock grazing. Dairying dominates the mixed farming economy in the northern part of the valley.

Many other Interior valleys have orchards and vegetable crops under irrigation. Dairying plays an important role in the valleys and trenches, where the fertile floodplains provide pasture and forage crops.

Interior Ranching

The physical nature of the southern Interior plateau is well-suited to livestock grazing. The plateau is deeply incised by the Fraser, North Thompson, Chilcotin, and Nicola Rivers, but much of the land lies above 1,000 metres, the upper limit for crop production in British Columbia. The grasslands and irrigated valleys are used for winter pasture and hay, while the uplands provide late spring and summer grazing on the forested rangeland (Figure 70). Half of the province's beef cattle population is raised there.

The range-cattle industry began with the demand for beef by prospectors in the gold fields. By 1887, ranches were established on all the best ranges of the southern Interior. Overgrazing was recognized as a problem by the turn of the century, but was eased temporarily because of heavy stock losses from a number of severe winters. By the 1920s, poor grazing practices, overstocking, and periodic droughts had ruined much of the grassland. Most of the damage was completed 40 to 100 years ago, although some ranges have deteriorated recently because of mismanagement. It should be noted that it takes from 10 to 50 years for a range to recover from prolonged overgrazing.

The number of beef cattle in B.C. has climbed steadily over the last 90 years (Figure 71). Presently, half the beef produced in British Columbia comes from Interior ranches. By the mid-1950s, the traditional grass-finishing of beef cattle declined because of growing competition from grain-fed Alberta beef. The B.C. ranchers converted to calf production and intensive feeding operations. Thus, British Columbia has turned into a net exporter of live cattle and an importer of beef: yearlings are raised in the Interior and sent to feeder enterprises in Alberta. Some Interior ranches have consolidated into larger units, but there are still many small operations. Another trend is the shift to part-time and guest ranches.

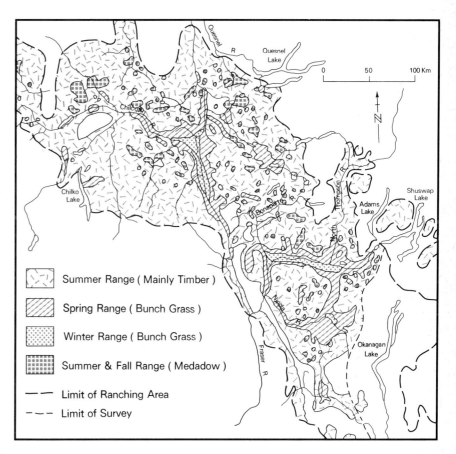

Most ranchers own their land and lease rangeland from the Crown. The cattle are grazed on permit and lease land at higher elevations during the summer months (Figure 70). Without this summer range, livestock production on private range and pasture land would not be economic. Winter range is confined to the lower valley sections and is privately owned.

The number of cattle permited on Crown range has increased over the past three decades, because logging of the Interior forests has created more grazing land. Because of the expansion of logging operations on Crown land and a growing recognition of wildlife values, conflicts have arisen between cattle grazing and other activities. The use of rangelands by cattle has lead to overgrazing and a deterioration of the wildlife habitat of elk and deer. The logging companies have claimed that cattle grazing also holds back tree regeneration on logged and burned-over forests. However, ranchers want to maintain their use of Crown land for grazing. Changes in land use on the Interior plateau are likely to occur as the beef market changes and as other activities compete for access to the forest rangelands.

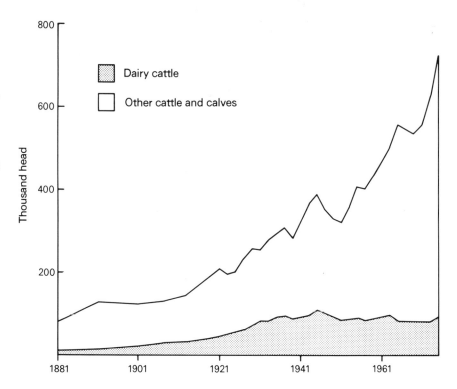

100

The Peace River District

Physically and economically, the northeastern plains of British Columbia are an extension of the Peace River district of Alberta. The growing season is short, but the fertile grassland soils support most of the grain produced in British Columbia. Wheat is the chief crop, but hogs and cattle are raised as well.

The first wave of agricultural settlers arrived after World War I. Veteran land grants and high wheat prices led to further expansion after World War II. The growth of the oil and gas industry in the 1950s provided a new market for farm products. In recent years, new agricultural land has been cleared along the Alaska Highway and near the rail extension from Fort St. John to Fort Nelson.

Nechako Pioneer Belt

The Nechako region (Figure 64) has severe cold spells in winter, and the harvests often fail because of heavy rainfall in late summer. Half the cultivated land is devoted to hay, but oats and wheat are grown as well. Dairying is important in the Prince George area, and vegetables are grown for the local market. Farming has not always been successful in this region, and many of the small-holders supplement their income by logging.

4 Fish and Wildlife

At the height of the last glaciation some 20,000 years ago, most of western Canada was covered by ice sheets and devoid of animal life. A few unglaciated areas such as the central and northern Yukon provided a refuge for a few hardy species, and the present-day animal populations are descendants of animals which migrated from these refuges after the retreat of the glaciers. Some crossed the Bering landbridge from Asia, others moved northward from the warmer, temperate regions of the present-day United States.

Each species has special environmental requirements for shelter, food and reproduction. Every physiographic, climatic and vegetation zone has distinctive fauna associated with it. The smaller animals are distributed according to vegetation zones, but some large predators such as the wolf have a broad geographical distribution.

Fish and wildlife provided the cornerstone of Indian hunting cultures in the Pacific Northwest. Salmon was a staple in the diet of coastal groups such as the Bella Coola and Nootka-Kwakiutl, and also played an important part in commercial and religious life. The coastal tribes also hunted seals, sea lions, sea otters, and whales, which supplied oil, food, and hides.

Hunting and Trapping

Fur-bearing animals were the first natural resource to be exploited by Europeans. The pursuit of beaver and the search for new trapping areas spurred exploration during the eighteenth and early nineteenth centuries. The accounts of fur traders, explorers, and missionaries provided the first detailed descriptions of the fauna.

Simon Fraser and David Thompson reported that beaver were plentiful west of the Rocky Mountains in the first decade of the nineteenth century, but trapping soon reduced their numbers. No attempt was made to leave breeding pairs to ensure a beaver population for the future. By 1900, overtrapping and the destruction of their habitat by expanding settlement had drastically reduced the beaver population of western Canada.

The influx of settlers and the introduction of European weapons had a disastrous effect on other fur-bearing animals as well. Logging and forest fires destroyed the woodland habitat of the caribou, marten, and fisher. The sea otter (*Enhydra lutris*) disappeared from the West Coast: their lustrous, thick pelts brought high prices in China during 150 years of ruthless exploitation. The sea otter had reached the verge of extinction by 1911, when an international treaty finally granted them protection. (A few sea otters were reintroduced to Vancouver Island from Amchitka Island, Alaska, in 1971.) Poisoning and trapping decimated the wolf and other animals regarded as agricultural pests. The Queen Charlotte Island caribou (*Rangifer tarandus dawsonii*) became extinct in 1935, as a result of overhunting from communities on the islands (Table 4).

Fortunately, in recent decades, the populations of some game and fur-bearing animals have increased. Moose (*Alces alces*) have spread farther west, and deer (*Odocoileus* species) have multiplied because of the new habitat created by forest clearances.

Source: Novakowski, N.S., 1970.
Canadian Field Naturalist,
Volume 84: 17-23.

Table 4: Extinct and endangered Wildlife Species

Species	Former Range	Present Range	Reason for Decline
Dawson caribou (*Rangifer tarandus dawsonii*)	Queen Charlotte Islands		Extinct about 1935 from over-hunting by local fishing communities
Roosevelt elk (*Cervus elaphus roosevelti*)	Southern British Columbia	A few on Vancouver Island	Overhunting
California bighorn sheep (*Ovis canadensis californiana*)	Southern Interior of British Columbia	Scattered herds	Hunting and competition from cattle
Vancouver Island wolf (*Canis lupus crassodon*)	Vancouver Island	Limited numbers	Reduction of habitat and early persecution
Wolverine (*Gulo gulo*)	Boreal forest	Northwestern Canada, seems to be declining	Overtrapping
Blue (glacier) bear (*Ursus americanus emmonsii*)	Southwest Yukon	Limited numbers	Overhunting
Caribou (*Rangifer tarandus*)	Tundra	Tundra	Overhunting and destruction of habitat by fires and logging
Sea otter (*Enhydra lutris*)	Coast of British Columbia	Small number reintroduced to Vancouver Island in 1971	Overhunting for furs

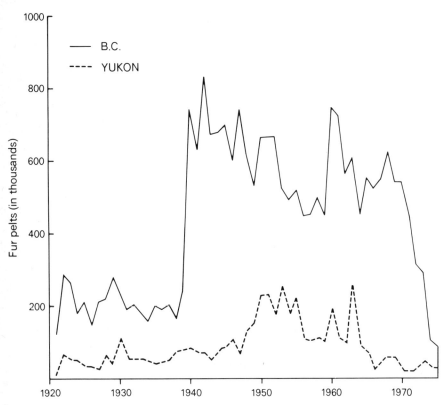

72 The number of fur pelts taken in British Columbia and Yukon Territory, 1920-1975. (Source: *Canada Year Book*, annual)

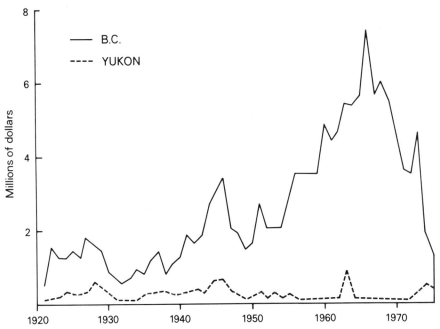

73 The value of furs trapped in British Columbia and Yukon Territory, 1920-1975. (Source: *Canada Year Book*, annual)

At present, more economic importance is attached to big-game (trophy) hunting than to the trapping of fur-bearing animals. Hunting and trapping have traditionally provided income for the native peoples. Indians and residents living off the land continue to hunt in order to supplement their meat supply, but the trapping of fur-bearing animals is declining. The fur yield is not controlled by the number of trappers, nor by animal populations, but by the vagaries of the fur market (Figures 72 and 73). There have been a series of slumps in recent decades, and trapping contributes little to the economies of British Columbia and the Yukon. Life on the winter trap-lines is hard, and higher incomes can be gained more easily in other occupations.

Big-game Hunting

Many residents hunt for meat, but many more join non-residents in recreational hunting for sport and the prestige of big-game trophies. Trophy-hunting, in particular, attracts increasing numbers of non-residents to the more remote areas of British Columbia and the Yukon. The Canadian Cordillera provides a major refuge for big-game species: it harbours most of the continental populations of mountain goats and sheep, grizzly bears, and mountain caribou. Cougars and wolves can still be found, even close to heavily populated areas. Moose, deer, elk, and black bear are very common.

Moose (*Alces alces*) is a highly valued trophy species, but it is often an important source of meat in the more remote areas of the north. There were no moose west of the Rocky Mountains until miners and settlers cleared forests by logging and fires. Since 1920, moose have extended their range westward to the Coast Range and now occupy most of British Columbia and the Yukon. Although considered a forest dweller, the moose usually avoids the monotonous coniferous forest in favour of aspen-birch groves and young second growth. Moose can often be seen browsing along lakeshores and in alder swamps during the summer months.

Deer (*Odocoileus* species) remains one of the most prolific game species in western Canada. In the early days, mule deer and whitetailed deer were an important source of food and hides. Deer populations increased as more forests were cleared. As in the case of moose, coniferous forests do not offer good deer habitat, as most of the forage has grown out of reach and the dense shade limits plant growth on the forest floor. The *mule deer* (*Odocoileus hemionus*) is widely distributed in British Columbia, except in the northwest, and is found in the Liard region of the Yukon. It inhabits open, second-growth coniferous forest and aspen parkland. In mountainous areas, the mule deer avoids areas of high snowfall and migrates to lower elevations in winter. The *whitetailed deer* (*Odocoileus virginianus*) occurs only in the southeastern portion of British Columbia, where it prefers cedar swamps and second-growth forest along stream banks.

The *elk* or wapiti (*Cervus elaphus*) is a popular game species which inhabits the open space of alpine meadows, aspen parkland, and river flats. It was widely distributed throughout the southern Interior prior to European settlement, but then suddenly disappeared from most of British Columbia. The elk now ranges from southern B.C., including Vancouver Island, to the northeastern portion of the province; it is found increasingly in areas where semi-open forest and grassland winter ranges offer a good habitat. The elk ranges from sea level up to about 2,300 metres. One subspecies found on northern Vancouver Island, the *Roosevelt Elk* (*Cervus elaphus roosevelti*), has declined because of disease and logging encroachment, but the population may be increasing slowly under government protection.

Caribou (*Rangifer tarandus*) was an important resource
for northern Indian groups before the arrival of European
explorers and settlers, and it has only recently been replaced
by other sources of food in the more remote areas. It
provided food, bedding, and lightweight warm clothing.
Caribou sinews were used for sewing thread, the bones as
tools, and the fat for light and heating. The native hunters
followed the nomadic herds of *barren-ground* (*R. arcticus*)
and *woodland (R. caribou) caribou*, which migrate between
seasonal pastures (Figure 74). The tundra summer range of
the barren-ground caribou may be 1,200 kilometres away
from their forested winter range. The *mountain caribou (R.
montanus)* does not move over such extensive distances, but
undertakes vertical seasonal migrations between high alpine
pastures and the lower forested slopes. The distribution of
caribou species is shown in Figure 74. The Dawson caribou
(*R. Tarandus dawsonii*) of the Queen Charlotte Islands has
been extinct since 1935.

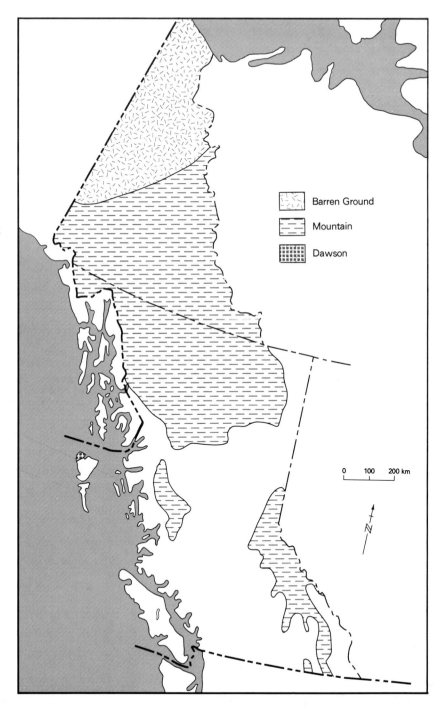

Barren Ground

Mountain

Dawson

0   100   200 km

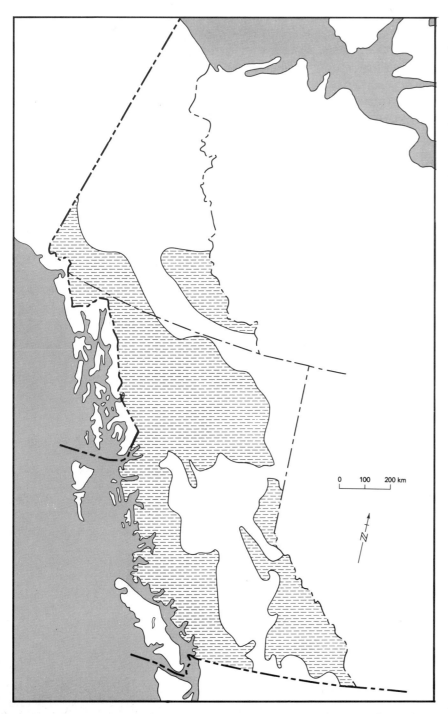

The *mountain goat (Oreamnos montanus)* is not really a goat but belongs to a group of mountain antelope. It inhabits the most rugged mountain terrain, and spends most of its time on steep grassy slopes at the base of cliffs, rocky ridges or high alpine pasture. The mountain goat can be found near sealevel on the coast and ranges up to the snowline as high as 2,300 metres (Figure 75). The Canadian Cordillera harbours about 80 per cent of the North American population of mountain goats. The mountain goat is avidly sought by trophy hunters. The meat is not considered palatable, so the hunter usually removes the head with its impressive horns and leaves the carcass to rot.

The *mountain-sheep* (*Ovis* species) is hunted for food by the northern native peoples and sought as a big-game trophy by sport hunters. The *Bighorn sheep (Ovis canadensis)* inhabits restricted alpine meadows in southern British Columbia. Two species, the Rocky Mountain and California bighorn sheep, have suffered seriously from encroaching settlement. They are critically dependent on the benchlands between 800 and 1,500 metres for winter range, but these areas are being taken over by domestic livestock. *Dall sheep (Ovis Dalli)* inhabits the alpine tundra of the mountain regions of northern British Columbia and the Yukon. It spends the summer months on rocky ridges and grassy slopes above 1,800 metres and descends to drier, south-facing slopes in winter. Its haunts are not very accessible, and the Dall's sheep population has not yet been decimated by hunting. Figure 76 shows the general distribution of mountain sheep populations.

The *bear* (*Ursus* species) is an important big game resource. The *black bear (Ursus americanus)* is common throughout British Columbia and the Yukon. It inhabits coniferous forest regions, where it prefers swamps and berry patches. Despite its reputation, three quarters of its diet consists of vegetable matter, but it can be a considerable nuisance, raiding garbage dumps and campsites for tempting morsels. It has very few natural enemies, apart from the grizzly and man. The *grizzly bear (Ursus arctos)* has gained the reputation of being the most dangerous and ferocious animal in North America. Very little is known about its everyday life, because it is extremely shy and avoids contact with man. However, the grizzly has been known to attack people when surprised and cornered, injured, or separated from its cubs. In earlier times, the grizzly was a dangerous quarry for native hunters armed only with primitive weapons, and this awesome animal became part of the totem culture of the Indians. Now the modern high-powered rifle has made this solitary species a target for trophy hunters. It is found throughout the mountain regions of British Columbia and the Yukon, but the total population is fairly small.

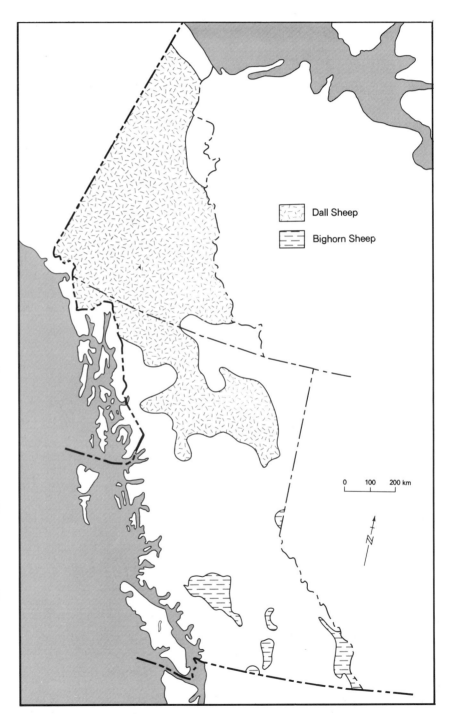

Dall Sheep

Bighorn Sheep

0   100   200 km

77 The regional distribution of resident
and non-resident hunting in British
Columbia (expressed as the
percentage of animals killed).
(Source: B.C. Dept. of Recreation and
Conservation, Fish and Wildlife
Branch, Study Report No. 2, 1968)

The *wolf (Canis lupus)* has only recently been recognized as a game animal rather than as a nuisance. It has few natural enemies, and even the grizzly will give way before a pack of wolves. The wolf is primarily a hunter of big-game: moose, deer, caribou, and mountain sheep. It follows the seasonal migrations of game from the high summer pastures down to the valleys in winter, preying on old or sick animals and young calves. The wolf ranges throughout most of British Columbia and the Yukon, but has been virtually exterminated in the south because of bounty-hunting and government predator-control programmes.

Small-game species such as the coyote and lynx occur in many areas, but they are hunted only lightly. Big-game animals are receiving the brunt of the hunting effort and pressure, because of the increased accessibility of remote regions. The number of licensed hunters has doubled in the last 25 years. Deer and moose harvests have expanded more than three and five times, respectively, during the same period. On the one hand, local residents have traditionally hunted for meat, and deer and moose still account for most of the game harvest. On the other hand, trophy hunting for caribou, mountain goat, and sheep represents a small proportion of the total. Most of the trophy hunters are inexperienced non-residents who fly into remote northerly areas for short visits. In general, the local and non-resident hunters do not conflict, because they pursue different game species with separate geographical distributions (Figure 77). However, conflicts can be expected to increase in southern British Columbia and the Kootenays, where the groups overlap. Non-resident hunters, most of them from the United States, are required to hire licensed guides. Guiding operations have grown rapidly since World War II, but most guides have alternative sources of income (prospecting, trapping or logging) to supplement their short seasonal work.

Sustained yield practices have been introduced in an attempt to prevent overhunting, which has threatened some species with extinction in the past. The hunting season and the size of harvest is restricted in areas with sparse game populations, and steps are being taken to protect the

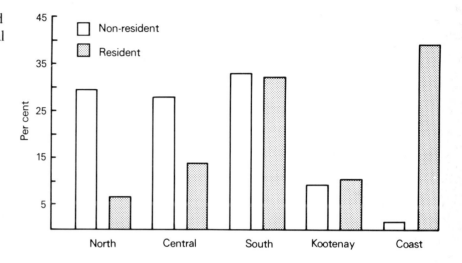

remaining habitat of endangered species. Most of this effort has been directed towards preserving the limited areas of winter range, which are critical for animal survival, but winter range is increasingly threatened by large-scale hydro developments. Hopefully, conservative measures will protect wildlife populations to the extent that future generations will be able to enjoy them alive rather than maintaining them as quarry for the trophy-hunters.

Commercial Fishing

More than twenty native species of fish are caught in the waters of the Pacific Northwest. The open ocean, the coastal waters, and the extensive network of lakes and rivers provide valuable breeding and feeding grounds for the fish. Much of the commercial fishing is concentrated along the coast off the mouths of salmon-spawning rivers and in the shallow waters of the continental shelf (Figure 78). Along Canada's West Coast, the shelf extends no more than 50 kilometres offshore. The sea yields a great variety of marine life, but salmon is the mainstay of the fishing industry, providing 70 per cent of the total catch in recent years (Figure 79). Herring and halibut are also important commercial species, although not as valuable as salmon. Bottom-dwellers such as sole, flounder, cod, and ocean perch contribute to the catch, but clams, oysters, crabs, and shrimps are also harvested by B.C. fishermen. Whaling and sealing once played a role in the West Coast fisheries, but are no longer part of the industry.

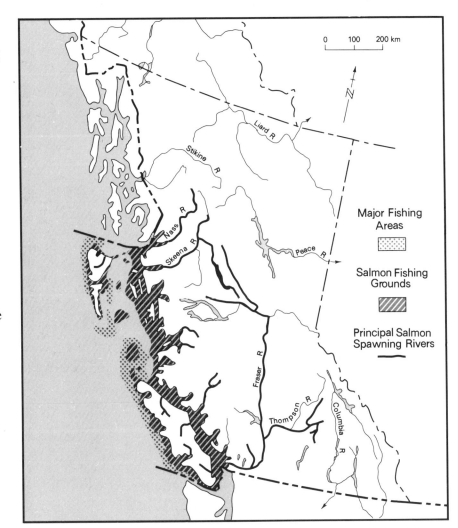

112

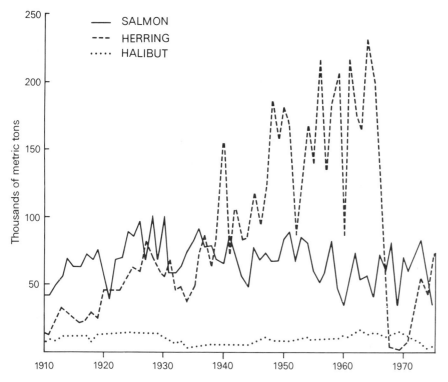

79 The volume of fish landed on the west
coast, by major species, 1910-1975.
(Sources: M.C. Urquhart and K.A.H.
Buckley, eds. *Historical Statistics of
Canada*, 1965 and Environment
Canada, Fisheries Service, *British
Columbia Catch Statistics,* annual)

Salmon

The salmon family includes steelhead, trout, and char, as
well as five species common to the West Coast: coho,
sockeye, pink, chum, and spring (chinook). The Pacific
salmon are anadromous: they breed and spend part of their
lives in freshwater before travelling to the ocean, where they
feed until maturity. Each of the five species has a different
life history. For example, pink salmon reach a weight of two
kilograms and live for two years, while the giant spring
salmon can live for as long as seven years and reaches over
50 kilograms.

The salmon are born from eggs laid in the gravel beds of
streams, 15 to 1,500 kilometres from the sea. After several
months, they emerge from the gravel as two-centimetre-long
fry. Depending on the species, they feed and grow in lakes or
rivers up to a year or more. Then, during the spring freshet,
the fingerlings head downstream to the sea, where they feed
and grow. The sockeye, pink, and chum feed on plankton
and tiny shrimp; the spring and coho eat smaller fish. After a
time, the salmon migrate back to their home streams,
struggling up to the spawning areas where they were born.
Sockeye and spring salmon are the strongest, migrating as
far as 1,500 kilometres upstream; other species spawn closer
to the sea. The salmon stop feeding once they enter
freshwater and die soon after spawning.

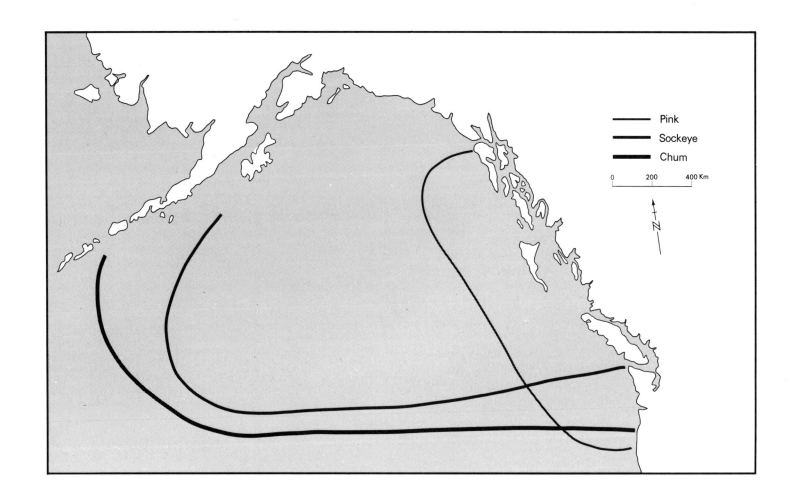

80 Limits of the ocean distribution for
    most of British Columbia's pink,
    sockeye and chum salmon.

Sockeye are the most valuable salmon because of their colour, flavour, and high oil content. Sockeye spawn in streams which have lakes in their watershed. The young would not survive unless they spent one to three years in a lake before migrating to the sea. Spawning runs occur between June and November, and each spawning area has a distinctive race. In spring, the young sockeye fingerlings leave their lake nurseries and move downstream to the sea, where they roam as far as the Gulf of Alaska and the north Pacific (Figure 80). Between the third and sixth years, they return to their spawning streams. Thus, the Fraser River sockeye are four-year fish, while the sockeye of the Skeena and Nass rivers range from four to six years at maturity. The Fraser River has the most important sockeye run in British Columbia and has been heavily exploited since the first cannery was established around 1860. The Skeena River run was important, but declined through overfishing in the early years of this century. It has since made a slow recovery.

Coho are a valuable commercial species and popular game fish. They migrate upriver in early fall and spawn in late November and December. Coho prefer streams close to the ocean, although some fish migrate 600 kilometres upstream. Unlike other species, the young fry stay in their spawning stream for a year, where they run the greatest risk from floods, droughts, pollution and predation. After a year, the fingerlings travel to the open ocean, where they feed for 18 months, reaching maturity when they are three years old.

Pink are the most widely distributed of all salmon. They live for two years and, with the exception of chums, spend the least amount of time in freshwater. They spend most of their time in the rich feeding areas of the Pacific Ocean. The adults leave the ocean in late summer and fall, when they begin to spawn in streams close to the sea.

Chum spawn in the lower tributaries along the Coast during the late fall. They rarely migrate more than 150 kilometres inland. The fry move directly to the sea, where they reach maturity in the third or fourth year.

Spring (chinook) are the largest and longest-living of the five salmon species. They migrate upriver throughout the year, but prefer the spring and fall months. The early runs make the longest journey, up to 1,500 kilometres, to their spawning areas. Most of the young fry move to the sea soon after hatching, but others stay in the lake or river for a year or more. Mature spring salmon range from three to seven years, but most of them are four or five years old when they return to spawn.

The death toll for all five salmon species is extremely high. For example, 3,000 eggs may be deposited by a sockeye, but only 100 will become fingerlings and travel to the sea. Of these, less than twenty will return as adults. Lethal changes in freshwater and ocean environments take the greatest toll of young fish; salmon are highly sensitive to changes in temperature and the oxygen content of water. High water temperatures in the spawning areas can inflict heavy damages, and fewer fry and fingerlings survive during low flow periods because of the fierce competition for food and living space. Silt and organic material (wood, bark) can cover the spawning beds and prevent food and oxygen from reaching the eggs. Water pollution, if sufficiently concentrated, can also kill fish.

The hazards facing the salmon in the spawning streams are well known, but it is more difficult to predict their chance of survival in the open ocean. There, too, abnormal water temperatures and poor light penetration can reduce their numbers. Birds and larger fish prey on the fry and fingerlings, while seals and killer whales feed on the mature fish.

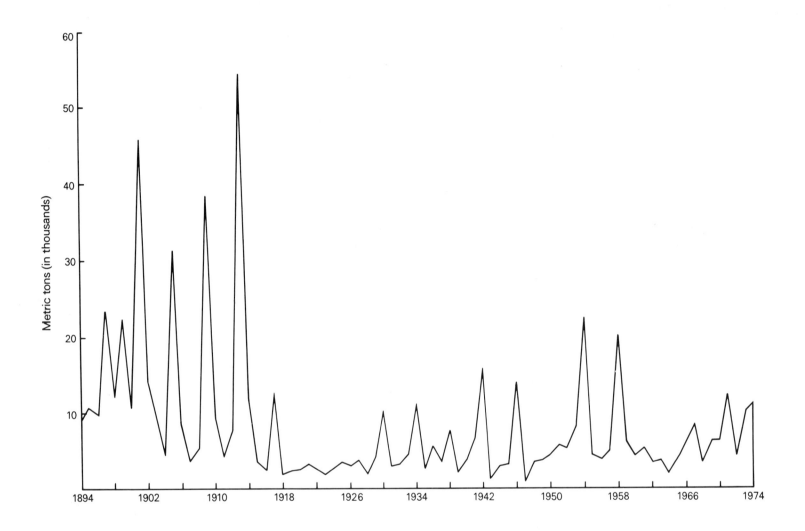

81 The Fraser River sockeye salmon pack, 1894-1974. Fraser River sockeye mature in a 4-year cycle; prior to 1914 the greatest catches were taken from the 1897-1901-1905-1909-1913 runs. After rockslides in Hell's Gate Canyon cut off access to spawning grounds, the big runs disappeared. (Source: International Pacific Salmon Fisheries Commission, annual reports)

Salmon became an important commercial product in the early nineteenth century, when salt-cured salmon was shipped to Hawaii and Asia. A canning industry developed on the lower Fraser River, near New Westminster, during the 1860s, and within ten years canneries appeared in increasing numbers on the Fraser and along the coast. By the turn of the century, there were more than seventy canneries between Steveston and Prince Rupert. Local and foreign markets were supplied with canned, smoked, and salted salmon. By 1900, sockeye salmon was the mainstay of the industry, forming almost 80 per cent of the average canned pack. Most of the sockeye salmon went up the Fraser River, which then was one of the greatest sockeye rivers in the world.

In the first decade of this century, the total catch by Canadian and American fishermen approached the limit of the sockeye run on the Fraser River, but within a few years disaster struck. Railroad builders, blasting a tunnel in the Fraser Canyon during 1913-14, caused a major rockslide which blocked the river at Hell's Gate. Sockeye and pink salmon were prevented from migrating to their upstream spawning areas in the Fraser watershed. The blockage was partly cleared in the following year, but the enormous runs had been permanently crippled (Figure 81).

The 1913 cycle had been the largest known on the Fraser River. The runs of 1897, 1901, 1905, 1909, and 1913 had provided more than half the total catch between 1897 and 1916. To this day, the four-year cycle has never recovered to its pre-slide volume, despite the construction of fishways at Hell's Gate that enable fish to bypass the block in their upstream migrations.

After the Fraser rockslide, the fishing industry began to make increasing use of the large runs in the northern rivers. As markets continued to grow, other salmon species began to replace the sockeye in importance. Pink and chum salmon packs increased and, since the 1920s, pinks have made up one third of the total pack. More than sixty per cent of the salmon is canned, and the rest is sold fresh, frozen, or smoked. Three quarters of the catch is taken by gillnetters; one quarter by seineboats and trollers (Figure 82). The

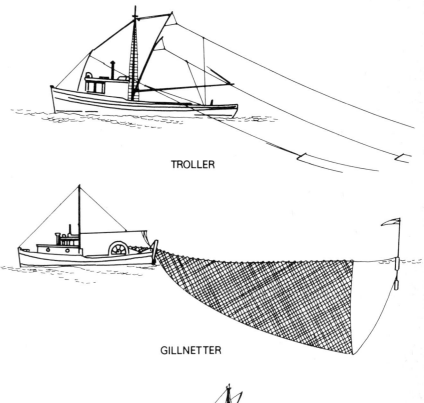

TROLLER

GILLNETTER

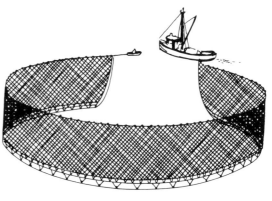

SEINEBOAT

seineboats are the largest salmon fishing vessels, but the short fishing season and high costs are cutting down their participation. Many of them spend their time in other fisheries (e.g. halibut and herring).

117

Competition became fierce in recent decades, as the demand grew and some of the runs declined. The number of fishermen has fallen over the past 50 years, but technological improvements in fishing vessels, gear, and navigational aids have increased the efficiency of individual boats. Since World War II, the use of electronic equipment such as echo sounders and radar, new synthetic materials for nets, and more reliable marine engines have had a major impact on the industry. Modern fleets can seriously deplete or even wipe out a salmon run within a few hours or days of fishing. The fishing seasons have been shortened and some fisheries shut down completely, in order to rehabilitate the stock.

Three major pressures face the salmon resource: overfishing, water pollution, and damage to fish habitats. Depletion of stocks by overfishing has been tackled by adopting a sustained yield policy, which regulates the number of licensed vessels, type of equipment, length of season, and size of catch. Fish habitats and spawning beds can be damaged by natural processes such as landslides and silting, but some of the greatest harm is caused by man's activities. Migration routes and spawning beds can be inhibited or destroyed by logging, landfill projects, mine tailings, erosion from urban land development, and hydro-electric dams.

A number of government programmes are aimed at protecting and restoring natural habitats, by ensuring that at least minimum flows are maintained on the rivers, and by introducing pollution controls. A second approach has been the enhancement of natural habitats by the construction of fishways, spawning channels, and hatcheries. Hatcheries short-circuit the freshwater stages of the young spring and coho salmon. Eggs from adult salmon are stripped by hand and reared under controlled temperature conditions. The fingerlings are then released into the stream and make their way to the sea, where they spend their adult life. Mature salmon return to their hatchery spawning area a few years later.

The travel and feeding habits of both native and hatchery fish are not fully understood, and the influx of hatchery fish into the ocean feeding grounds may well increase the stiff

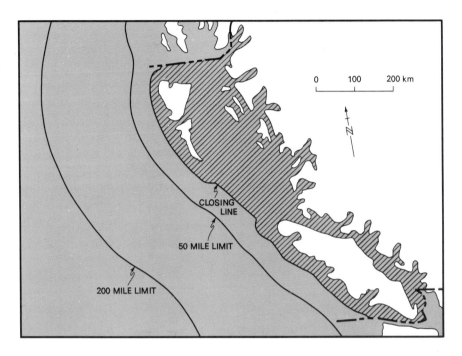

competition among native fish for survival. At the moment, the hatcheries are bringing high returns of mature salmon, but the long-term impact of the newcomers remains to be seen.

A major problem is that fishery resources migrate across international boundaries. American boats fish for Fraser sockeye in Juan de Fuca Strait, and Canadian fishermen catch Columbia River salmon farther south. In 1937, the International Pacific Salmon Fisheries Commission was founded by the Canadian and United States governments in order to share the Fraser River salmon, which travel through U.S. waters before spawning in B.C. rivers. At first, the treaty dealt with sockeye only, but has been extended to include pink salmon. Under the terms of the treaty, the Fraser catch is divided equally between American and Canadian fishermen. In addition, controls are maintained to ensure that the catch and spawning escapement are balanced.

In 1953, both countries signed an agreement with Japan, establishing the International North Pacific Fisheries Commission (NORPAC). This was also designed to protect the salmon runs from depletion. Japan now fishes for Alaskan and Asian salmon runs west of 170 degrees longitude.

Fishing upon the high seas has had a strong tradition of freedom: after all, no one could claim to own the fish. As competition intensified, some countries took steps to set exclusive fishing zones off their own shores (Figure 83). This was not entirely successful, because the fish ranged far beyond these limits where they could be overfished by the fleets of other nations. As signs of depletion became too obvious to be ignored, international treaties were signed in an attempt to prevent further damage.

Herring

This species has been fished fairly regularly off the West Coast since 1877. Seining for herring began early, but most of the catch was used as halibut bait rather than for human consumption. A salt herring industry was established at the turn of the century, but exports of salt herring declined in the 1930s. In 1924, a reduction industry was set up to convert herring into oil and fish-meal; within a few years, the whole catch was used in this process. The herring fishery was closed for four years in 1969 to allow the badly depleted stocks to recover (Figure 79). However, it re-opened in 1971, with the restriction that herring be caught for human consumption only. Herring fishing has become a rapidly-expanding industry which supplies its major market, Japan, with herring roe and fillets.

Halibut

Halibut has been fished commercially since 1888. The main feeding grounds lie off the west and north coasts of Vancouver Island, Queen Charlotte Sound, and Hecate Strait. Halibut are still caught by long-line: a series of hooked lines which rest on the ocean bottom. The halibut industry became valuable with the completion of the transcontinental railroad; halibut, unlike salmon, cannot be canned, so it needed quick transport to reach markets.

For the first 25 years, halibut fishing was free of any restrictions on the length of season, size or location of the catch, or the size of fish. As a result, large quantities of immature fish were taken, and spawning banks were destroyed. Halibut have a limited distribution and are slow to mature (12 years for the female). The main halibut banks have bottom temperatures of 3 to 8 degrees Celsius; outside this range, the fish are scattered and the catch is poor. The concentrated banks were easy to overfish, and too few young fish were left to mature and spawn. Serious concerns were voiced in 1915, and the United States and Canada attempted to reach an agreement to protect and manage the halibut yield. The International Halibut Convention was signed and the work of the International Pacific Halibut Commission began in 1923. A closed season was adopted in place of year-round fishing. In 1949, trawling for halibut was banned. By 1954, the halibut season had been reduced to 21 days, catch limits were imposed, and spawning grounds closed to fishermen. Despite these measures, the dangers of overfishing and depletion remain. Halibut stocks are currently being heavily fished by Japanese and Soviet factory ships in north Pacific waters. Canada's share of the Pacific catch has increased while the United States catch has declined over the last 30 years.

Sealing

The hunting of seals began in the 1860s off the west coast of Vancouver Island. The Indians had long been intercepting herds of seals travelling north to their rookeries in the Pribilof Islands. By the middle of the nineteenth century, European traders were encouraging the hunt. Victoria became the home port of the sealing fleet, which expanded and moved farther afield to hunting grounds close to the rookeries in the Bering Sea. Fierce competition developed with American sealers from Alaska; vessel and cargo seizures by the Americans and Russians led to tense relations with Canadian sealers. A treaty was signed between the United States and Great Britain in 1893, which banned the Canadian sealing fleet from the Bering Sea. The attempt at protection was unsuccessful, and the herds of the North Pacific were decimated. Eventually, Japan and Russia signed an agreement, and the Pacific was closed to commercial sealing operations.

Whaling

The whaling industry began in the 1830s, when New England whalers appeared in the Pacific Northwest. Before then, the Nootka Indians had hunted whales off the coast of Vancouver Island. Five species were commercially valuable: the gray, finback, humpback, blue (the largest), and the sperm whale. In the mid-nineteenth century, the New England whalers retreated; it was no longer profitable to hunt whales over such long distances. In addition, the price of whale oil had fallen because of growing competition from petroleum as a source of lamp oil.

However, a market for whale products persisted; whale oil was still used as a lubricant, food and especially, fertilizer. A local industry sprang up, and shore stations were established along the west coast of Vancouver Island and on the Queen Charlotte Islands. By 1946, the International Whaling Convention was drawn up to protect remaining herds from extinction. Since 1972, commercial whaling has been banned in Canada, but international efforts to restrict whaling on the world's oceans have not been successful.

Sport Fishing

The marine and freshwaters of British Columbia and the rivers and lakes of the Yukon offer excellent opportunities for sport fishing. Salmonids are the most important game fish in western Canada: trout, char, and salmon (coho and spring). In addition, whitefish and grayling are caught in northern B.C. and the Yukon.

Most of the salmon fishing is concentrated in the Strait of Georgia. Some cod and flounder are caught, but represent a very small fraction of the total saltwater catch. The harvesting of clams and oysters is popular in intertidal areas where the shellfish beds have not been closed as a result of sewage contamination or invasions of red tide (a toxic marine organism). Sport fishermen are beginning to express growing concern about congestion, over-fishing, and pollution in the Strait of Georgia. Many are calling for more intensive fisheries management and stricter controls on activities which pollute or damage wildlife habitats. The hatchery programme of British Columbia has been designed to cater to the sport fishermen in the coastal waters: coho, spring, and steelhead are the major species reared.

The most popular freshwater species in B.C. are trout and char. Rainbow trout is the single most important freshwater sport fish, found everywhere except the Liard Basin. Steelhead is found in most of the larger streams of the mainland coast of British Columbia and Vancouver Island. Cut-throat trout is fished by resident anglers on the coast and, to a lesser extent, in the Kootenays. Dolly Varden and lake trout are common in most of the Interior lakes north of the Okanagan.

In recent years sport fishing has increased rapidly in the northern British Columbia and the Yukon; new roads have opened up previously inaccessible lakes and streams. Much of the growth has been linked with the expanding tourist industry, and many of the new fishermen are non-residents. Arctic char competes with trout and salmon (spring and chum) for popularity among the northern anglers. The commercial freshwater fishery of the Yukon has always been small, because of the limited number of inland lakes.

5 Parks and Recreation

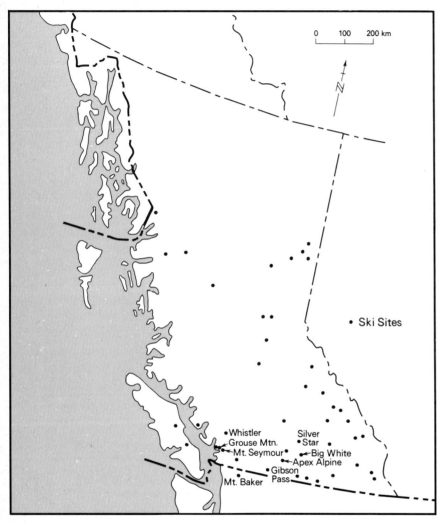

0 100 200 km

• Ski Sites

• Whistler
Silver
• Grouse Mtn. • Star
• Mt. Seymour • • Big White
Apex Alpine
• Gibson
Mt. Baker Pass

British Columbia and the Yukon have an enormous potential for outdoor recreation and, although some sites close to major towns and cities are overcrowded, many recreational resources remain untouched. In the early days, few roads penetrated the mountains, transportation services were limited, and few people had the money or time to travel far from their own communities. However, during the last two decades, a growing urban population with more income, leisure time, and mobility has created a massive demand for outdoor recreation.

The travel industry has taken advantage of the greatly extended highway network of western Canada. By the late 1960s, tourism ranked second only to mining in the Yukon economy as travelling conditions improved on the unpaved Alaska Highway. Many people are attracted by the scenic beauty of the north, by the opportunities to hunt and fish, and by the chance to explore the historic sites of the Klondike gold rush. The expansion of the road network in the Interior of British Columbia over the last two decades has also made many remote areas accessible to travellers in search of natural scenery and their historical heritage.

Private and chartered aircraft are opening up remote wilderness areas to hikers, hunters, fishermen, and skiers. Between 1972 and 1975, the number of non-commercial pilot licences held in British Columbia increased by 30 per cent. Pleasure boats have brought extensive stretches of the coast within easy reach of more and more people; more than 110,000 pleasure boats are now owned by residents of the Strait of Georgia region. Boating has grown to such an extent that there is a shortage of moorage and marinas along the southern coast of British Columbia.

One of the most rapidly growing activities is *skiing*. Cross-country skiers seek out quiet logging roads and wilderness trails, while alpine skiers head for the 70 facilities operating in British Columbia (Figure 84). Weekend skiers use areas close at hand and visit slopes best suited to their ability. The vacation skier may travel much farther in search of challenging slopes or regions where dry powder snow is consistently available.

The major alpine skiing regions include the southern Coast Mountains, the southern Interior, and the Kootenays. Eight areas account for most of the skiing activity at present: Whistler Mountain, Mount Seymour, Grouse Mountain, and Gibson's Pass (Manning Park), all within easy reach of the Lower Mainland; and Apex Alpine, Big White, and Silver Star in the Interior.

The operating season varies widely according to relief and climate, but the average length is 140 days a year. The slopes of the southern Coast Mountains are used intensively by day skiers and weekend skiers living in the Lower Mainland region. However, moderate winter temperatures and invasions of moist Pacific air can bring unfavourable snow conditions. The continental climate of the southern Interior provides abundant dry powder snow at higher elevations, and skiers can enjoy clear, sunny weather in midwinter. All the important ski areas in the Interior are located above 1,000 metres. Some ski slopes can have as much as ten metres of snowfall during the winter months. As on the coast, the slopes range from gentle trails to challenging runs for the advanced skier.

The Kootenays offer good snow conditions and favourable weather during the ski season. Helicopter skiing began in the Bugaboo Mountains of the Purcell Range in 1965 and has since spread to the Cariboo and Monashee regions of the Interior. Helicopters have also brought virgin snow and glacier runs within easy reach of Vancouver skiers.

The northern Interior and the Yukon are handicapped by shorter winter days, extremely cold weather, and low relief. Alpine skiing facilities have been developed to serve some communities such as Smithers and Prince George, but the future lies in cross-country skiing.

Source: *Canada Year Book*, 1972.

In summer, busy highways and crowded campsites are an indication of the pressure on other recreational resources. There are heavy demands on fish and wildlife stocks close to major towns. For example, sport fishing and hunting have grown to such an extent that intensive management schemes are being introduced in the lower Fraser valley. Summer cottage development on the Gulf Islands reached such a pitch that in 1969 the provincial government introduced a freeze on subdivisions of less than four hectares until proper community plans could be drawn up.

Given reasonable care, recreational resources are renewable as long as conflicting demands are kept to a minimum. Logging, mining, and urban sprawl are often cited as the major causes of conflict, but recreational activities themselves can also inflict damage. For instance, cross-country skiers seeking quiet enjoyment object to snowmobilers using the same trails.

As more people explore the countryside for recreational enjoyment, conflicts with other resource uses will intensify; proposals to allow mining and logging within provincial parks have been fairly common. Unfortunately, the value of recreational experiences is often downgraded because it cannot be expressed in dollars: the money spent on camping or skiing equipment, boats, fishing tackle, guns and ammunition does not reflect the full value of outdoor recreation.

Earlier in this century, nobody worried about the real value of outdoor recreation because there seemed to be an unlimited supply of land and resources for all purposes. Now that logging and mineral exploration are moving into previously untouched areas, the pressure to preserve recreational land is growing.

National and Provincial Parks

Two themes have underlain the creation of parks in western Canada: the conservation of areas with spectacular scenery and threatened wildlife, and the attempt to encourage tourism and provide opportunities for outdoor recreation. The first Canadian national parks were established in the Rocky Mountains soon after the completion of the transcontinental railroads. Banff Hot Springs (Alberta) was declared a reserve in 1885. In the following year, Glacier and Yoho were set aside as land reserves in British Columbia (Table 5). Both were declared National Parks after the Dominion Forest Reserves and Park Act was passed by the Canadian Parliament in 1911. Later on, two more scenic areas were set aside through an agreement between the governments of Canada and British Columbia: Mount Revelstoke (1914) and Kootenay (1920). This marked the end of national park creation in B.C. and the Yukon until the 1970s, when Pacific Rim and Kluane were set aside (Figure 85).

Table 5:
National parks in British Columbia and the Yukon Territory

Date Established	Park	Size (sq. km.)
1886	Glacier	8,390
1886	Yoho	8,165
1914	Mount Revelstoke	1,610
1920	Kootenay	8,744
1970	Pacific Rim	2,415
1972	Kluane	136,870
		166,194

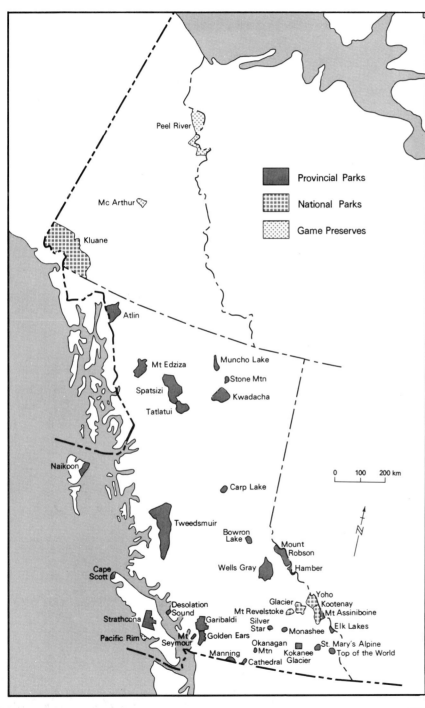

85 The distribution of major parks and game preserves in British Columbia and Yukon Territory.

Legend (map):
- Provincial Parks
- National Parks
- Game Preserves

Map labels:
Peel River, Mc Arthur, Kluane, Atlin, Mt Edziza, Muncho Lake, Stone Mtn, Spatsizi, Kwadacha, Tatlatui, Naikoon, Carp Lake, Tweedsmuir, Bowron Lake, Mount Robson, Wells Gray, Hamber, Cape Scott, Desolation Sound, Glacier, Yoho, Kootenay, Strathcona, Mt Revelstoke, Mt Assiniboine, Garibaldi, Silver Star, Elk Lakes, Pacific Rim, Mt Seymour, Golden Ears, Monashee, Manning, Okanagan Mtn, Kokanee Glacier, St. Mary's Alpine, Top of the World, Cathedral

0 100 200 km

The first national parks were established in an attempt to foster tourism; they were regarded as economic assets, rather than as wilderness reserves. Railroad companies planned resorts similar to Banff, but many of these proposals were unsuccessful. For example, ultimate development in Glacier National Park was limited to trails and alpine huts for climbers and alpinists. Until 1962, the railway provided the only means of access to this park.

Although the intent was to protect areas of outstanding scenery, resource exploitation was permitted within the early national parks. Activities such as mining and logging were not considered a threat to recreational enjoyment; a lead mine operating east of Field since the 1880s was allowed to continue when the area became part of the Yoho reserve in 1902 (the mine eventually closed down). Similarly, Glacier Park had originally been set aside as a forest reserve, but large lumber leases were upheld long after the area had acquired park status. Leases on the verge of being re-activated have been purchased by the federal government over the past ten years to prevent logging in this park.

Beginning in 1911, the British Columbia government set aside a series of wilderness parks which, by the mid-1940s, encompassed over 40,000 square kilometres. Strathcona Provincial Park was created in 1911, followed by Mount Robson in 1913 and Garibaldi in 1920. These early provincial parks were modelled after the national parks. They, too, were conceived as resorts or tourist attractions rather than as wilderness areas. The example of Banff was to be followed, with motor roads, cabins and hotels.

However, B.C. provincial parks remained undeveloped, largely inaccessible, unused, and virtually unknown by the public during the 1910s and 20s. The original provincial parks had been protected from resource development in order to enhance their attractiveness. In later years, as they failed to produce the expected revenues, it became difficult to justify the parks on solely economic terms.

By the late 1920s, pressure from resource industries had led to a relaxation of the protective legislation. The depletion of accessible resources in British Columbia raised the value of the timber and minerals within parks. In the late 1930s, new legislation allowed multiple use in most of the large provincial parks. Two new park classifications were introduced: Class A parks, in which land and timber were protected but mining claims allowed; and Class B parks, in which multiple use was permitted, except where recreation values would be damaged. This concept of multiple use was interpreted broadly, and many parks were opened up for resource development. Parks could also be reclassified, reduced in area, or cancelled outright.

Giving assurances that resource exploitation would not be banned from provincial parks, the government added enormous new areas to the park system. After a gap of 15 years, the provincial park area was increased sixfold and, between 1938 and 1944, four huge parks were created, totalling over 36,000 square kilometres: Tweedsmuir, Wells Gray, Hamber and Liard River. Manning Park was set aside during the same period. The idea of encouraging tourism and opening up the north underlay the creation of many of the new areas, which were largely designated as Class B parks. The Liard River Park was, in fact, cancelled in 1948 after only four years of existence.

The grand-resort concept of parks disappeared after World War II. The large parks had received only limited development and remained largely inaccessible. Major reductions in park area took place between 1952 and 1972; the provincial park system shrank from 45,000 to 26,000 square kilometres. The six large wilderness parks created prior to 1945 still accounted for over 80 per cent of the total provincial park area.

Resource developments began to encroach on previously remote parkland. For example, until 1954, Tweedsmuir was one of the largest protected wilderness areas in North America. However, boundary revisions since the construction of the Nechako Dam reduced its area by over 4,000 square kilometres. In 1954, with the hydro-electric development at Kitimat, the water level of several lakes within the northern portion of the park was raised: Ootsa, Whitesail, Eutsuk and Tetachuck. The timber was not cleared before flooding, so lakeshores were converted into impassable, waterlogged jungles.

The idea that any restrictions on resource use would be a threat to prosperity was held firmly. However, there was a slow shift toward the consideration of values other than economic ones. In 1965, the B.C. Parks Act gave the Lieutenant-Governor-in-Council the power to create parks and recreation areas on all Crown lands. The park classification system was revised to include three categories:

Class A: recreation only (e.g. Mount Robson, Garibaldi)

Class B: multiple use allowed, except where resource use would be detrimental to recreation (e.g. Tweedsmuir)

Class C: small local parks for intensive recreation (e.g. Silver Star, Apex Mountain)

The act also created two other land classifications: Nature Conservancies, which could be established within parks to protect certain areas from heavy use; and Recreation Areas, which could be set aside to act as buffers around existing parks. Recently created Recreation Areas include buffer zones around Mount Edziza and Atlin provincial parks.

A major expansion in the provincial park system began in 1972. In northern British Columbia, Mount Edziza was designated as a Class A park in late 1972. This fascinating landscape of young volcanic cones, ash falls and lava flows is now fully protected. Ten new Class A parks were created in 1973, many of them in northern British Columbia where few parks had existed in the past: Kwadacha Wilderness, Tatlatui, Atlin, Carp Lake, Naikoon, Cape Scott, Desolation Sound, St. Mary's Alpine, Top of the World, and Elk Lakes. These parks were chosen to protect either characteristic or unique natural environments. Some of them represent fragile subalpine or tundra settings, other thriving coastal plant and animal communities threatened by human intrusion.

In 1975, the provincial government created the Spatsizi Plateau Wilderness Park, which includes sparkling lakes and open table-lands. Spatsizi was set aside to alleviate hunting pressures on the area's mountain sheep, goats and caribou.

Even with the recent expansion, the provincial park area now covers less than five per cent (approximately 50,000 square kilometres) of British Columbia. The park system is made up of nine major parks: Tweedsmuir, Strathcona, Mount Edziza, Spatsizi, Atlin, Garibaldi, Mount Robson, Wells Gray and Kwadacha Wilderness; two dozen intermediate-sized parks; and many small parks providing campsites, picnic grounds, or protection for single outstanding recreational attractions.

Changes have also been taking place in the national parks system of western Canada. The creation of the two new national parks has brought renewed conflict between resource development and wilderness preservation. In 1970, three areas on the west coast of Vancouver Island were set aside as Pacific Rim National Park. The three sections include Long Beach, the Broken Islands group, and the West Coast Trail between Banfield and Port Renfrew. Long Beach, in particular, has been under heavy recreational pressure in recent years. The fedeal government decided that one solution to the problem of congestion would be to declare the area a National Park and thus restrict motor vehicle access. The Broken Islands have escaped recreational development because of their isolation, but the populations of seals, sea lions and bird colonies are now protected within the park. The West Coast Trail, which winds through 70 kilometres of rain forest, is preserved as a historic monument. It was constructed early in this century as a life-saving route for sailors shipwrecked along the treacherous west coast of Vancouver Island. At present, trails, campgrounds and information services have been developed only at Long Beach.

Pacific Rim Park itself took many years to become established because of boundary disputes. Around 1930, the federal government asked that a large section of the coastline be set aside for eventual designation as a national park. However, mounting pressure from resource industries in the late 1940s led to an opening up of the reserve for logging and private ownership. The provincial government finally arranged to acquire the land, which was then turned over to the federal government for administration as a national park. Problems between the government and logging companies holding long-term leases in the area were eventually resolved, and this stretch of coast was designated as a park in 1970.

Similar conflicts have arisen during the creation of Kluane National Park in the southwest Yukon. The area had been placed in park reserve in 1942 in order to protect local populations of mountain goat, sheep, caribou, and grizzly bear. The Canadian Parliament first approved the creation of Kluane National Park in 1972, but the plan met with strong opposition from mining groups and local commercial interests.

The major obstacle has been potential hydro-power, copper, gold, and other mineral deposits which have been mined sporadically, though with limited economic gain. Nevertheless, their presence has brought about the exclusion of about 5,200 square kilometres of original reserve from the park: Kluane Lake and the plateau country to the north, which is important for caribou and other wildlife species.

Most of the wildlife is concentrated in the Kluane Range immediately west of the Alaska Highway, where most of the mineral claims have been located. The high peaks and icefields of the St. Elias Range lie behind these front ranges, and only glimpses of them can be caught from the highway. The St. Elias massive is a huge area of rock and ice, with eight peaks of over 5,000 metres, rising from one of the world's largest non-polar icefields. Man has hardly penetrated these rugged mountains, which occupy most of Kluane National Park. Mount Logan (5,950 metres), Canada' highest mountain, was first scaled in 1925, but hundreds of other peaks remain unclimbed.

Although relatively few people have explored Kluane as yet, other national and provincial parks are extremely popular with recreationists. Visits to provincial parks have doubled over the last ten years. More than ten million visits were made to B.C. parks in 1975, about one fifth of them by overnight campers. The most heavily used areas are Mount Seymour, Cultus Lake, and Golden Ears, which are all close to Vancouver. The older-established National Parks in British Columbia have each received over one million visitors a year recently. Their growth in popularity has been enormous: 853,000 people visited Kootenay National Park in 1970, compared to 28,000 in 1945. Mount Revelstoke, Glacier and Yoho have experienced similar increases, and visitors to Pacific Rim National Park now exceed 400,000 a year.

Ecological Reserves

During an earlier period, game preserves were established in the Yukon Territory to protect unique or endangered wildlife species. For example, the McArthur Game Preserve was set aside to protect what was once considered a distinct species on the verge of extinction: the Fannin (saddle-backed) sheep. This particular mountain sheep is now known to be the result of interbreeding between Dall (white) sheep and Stone (black) sheep.

British Columbians relied on their provincial park system to protect threatened wildlife populations but, since hunting was allowed in many areas, these conservation measures were not entirely successful. Biologists expressed concern that special protection be given to samples of B.C.'s natural diversity. Pressure grew in the mid-1960s, encouraged by the introduction of the ten-year International Biological Programme. One of the aims of scientists involved in this programme has been to identify and preserve samples of the world's biological communities for research and education. A number of sites in British Columbia and the Yukon Territory were identified as part of this effort.

No action has been taken to date in the Yukon, but in 1971 the Ecological Reserves Act of British Columbia was passed by the provincial legislature. The main purpose of the act is to set aside ecological reserves which will serve as:
1) outdoor laboratories for biological research
2) benchmark areas, with which to compare changes taking place elsewhere
3) gene pools, to maintain genetic and ecological diversity
4) outdoor classrooms for students of natural history

Educational and scientific uses are encouraged under permit. Mineral exploration, logging, cattle grazing, camping and fishing are not allowed. These areas are not intended as recreational attractions: the public is not prohibited, but access is not encouraged. Many of the reserves created to date lie in remote areas. Most are ordinary samples of common plant and animal communities, which do not attract much public interest.

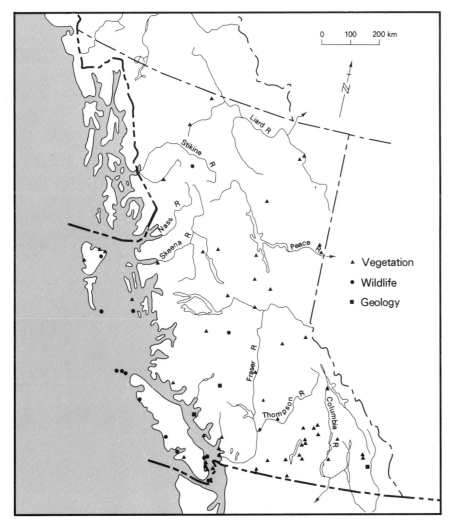

Legend (map):
- ▲ Vegetation
- ● Wildlife
- ■ Geology

So far, more than seventy ecological reserves have been established in the province, covering a total of 800 square kilometres. Many are small areas protecting representative samples of typical plant and animal communities, as well as unique or rare biological features. At first, many of the sites selected lay in the southern half of the province, but most of the recent acquisitions are in northern British Columbia. The reserves range from colonies of marine mammals and sea birds on offshore islands to plant and forest communities scattered throughout the province (Figure 86). A few geological sites have also been protected, including the hot springs at Ram Creek in the Kootenays. The largest area is the Gladys Lake Ecological Reserve within Spatsizi Plateau Provincial Park. Although hunting is currently allowed within the park, it is not permitted in the reserve, which covers 332 square kilometres and protects Stone sheep, mountain goats and their environment.

Reserves protecting rare plant communities or sea bird colonies may be very small, but large areas are needed to protect viable populations of mountain goats, sheep, caribou or grizzly bears. Winter range and breeding grounds are the key to the survival of these species. Some of the big-game ranges are so large that it is impossible to place them within a single ecological reserve. Protection is possible within some of the larger provincial parks, but it would be more practical if more enlightened land and wildlife management practices were adopted in regions outside parks.

There is also provision within the Ecological Reserves Act to set aside natural environments which have been modified by man. The idea underlying this part of the act is to study the recovery of altered areas. Some reserves already include logged, overgrazed, or burned areas; eventually, disturbed sites such as mine tailings will be included in the reserve system.

Historical Resources

The history of western Canada, although short, is extremely colourful and almost entirely tied to the exploitation of natural resources. Settlements around fur-trading posts, mining camps, mill towns and supply centres fulfilled the function of way-stations for resources on their way outside. Depending upon the revenue coming in, some of the camps became real towns, others reverted to ghost towns.

World markets for timber, copper and gold had a profound effect upon everybody's life in these frontier settlements. Booms followed busts, feverish building gave way to quiet periods of decay, and every decade produced its own set of old-timers. The history of British Columbia and the Yukon is not one of monuments erected by nameless thousands for the wealthy few; it is recorded in the cabins, long-toms, and trams of the miner who fought against the odds of weather, mountains and transportation. This is the legacy of struggle, triumph, and defeat. Only by walking through an old mining camp, touching the rails of an abandoned spur line, or drifting through the rapids of wild rivers can Canadians understand their past. Museums and books can give a first insight, but much is still there to be seen at first hand, and it must be saved.

Rivers are being dammed regardless of their function as the arteries of our history. Old settlements are torn apart in the flurry of development. Action can and must be taken to preserve much of this heritage, built by people of many nations and ethnic origins. These remnants document one of the most fascinating stories of the last century.

Some initial steps have been taken. Dawson City was declared a National Historic Site in 1969. The old stern-wheeler, the S.S. *Keno*, and buildings such as the Palace Grand Theatre have been restored as part of the effort to preserve this northern gold-rush town. Canada and the United States have proposed that the Chilkoot Pass be set aside as an international park commemorating the many thousands who travelled from Skagway to the Klondike gold fields at the turn of the century. Some thought is also being given to protecting the Yukon River and the remaining cabins along its bank, which preserve memories of the gold-mining and trapping days. Fort Langley, a Fraser valley trading post founded in 1850, has been partially restored and designated a National Historic Site; it was there that the Colony of British Columbia was proclaimed in 1858. Barkerville, the centre of the Cariboo gold rush, has been declared a Provincial Historic Park, and the restored buildings are a popular tourist attraction in the summer months. A few other localities in the province, including old mining camps and forts, are also preserved as historic parks, but many sites still remain unprotected.

6 Natural Hazards

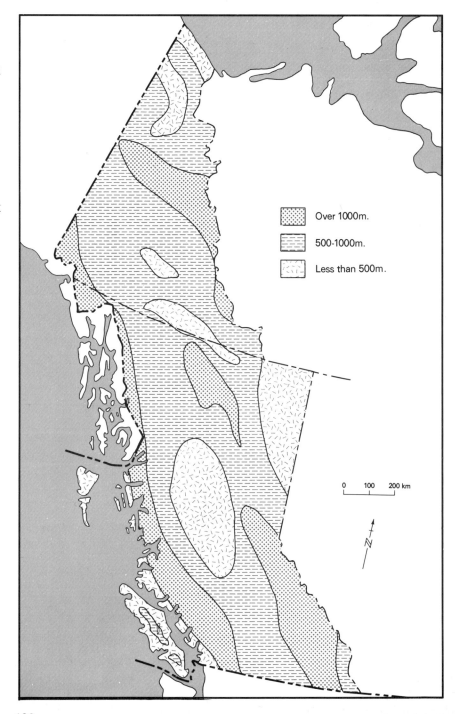

Landslides, avalanches, floods, and earthquakes are natural events in the development of the physical landscape; they become hazards only when people move into the threatened area. With mining, logging, and recreational developments in mountainous regions, more people are exposed to the risk of devastating landslides and avalanches. Floods can inflict major damage when communities expand onto floodplains, which are very attractive for urban and industrial schemes. There have been no major losses from earthquakes in British Columbia and the Yukon, because most tremors have occurred in uninhabited areas.

The incidence of natural hazards in western Canada is not really known. The tendency is to underestimate how frequent and widespread they are, because many regions are sparsely populated. For example, the real extent of losses from forest fires and invasions of pests and diseases is unknown. Even in areas that have a long history of settlement, records have been kept only since the turn of the century. Most of the known deaths and property damage have been caused by landslides, floods, and avalanches, which have killed more than fifty people in the last ten years. As the population grows, the losses will increase, and while in some cases the only option is to avoid hazardous areas, steps can be taken to reduce the threat of damage. Floods and avalanches occur every year, and the risk can be assessed by seasonal observations over a long period of time. Areas susceptible to earthquakes, landslides, and forest fires can be identified although predicting precisely when and where they will occur, is not yet possible.

Over 1000m.

500-1000m.

Less than 500m.

0   100   200 km

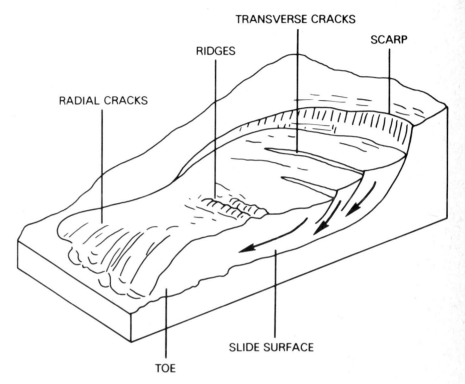

88 A simplified diagram showing the major features of a landslide.

Landslides

Large-scale landslides are common in any mountainous region. In the Alps and Andes, for example, villages built on the floors of steep-sided valleys are sometimes destroyed by sliding masses of rock set loose without any warning. Signs of ancient rockslides can be traced throughout the Canadian Cordillera, and disasters such as the Frank Slide (Alberta, 1903) warn of the potential toll as people continue to penetrate areas of high relief (Figure 87). Some slides consist entirely of rock material, others of soil only, and some are mixtures of rock, soil, and ice. They can range from small slumps of a few metres to gigantic slides.

Old *rockslides* are recognizable when travelling through mountainous country: a steep scarp marks the point from which the rock face broke away (Figure 88). A jumbled mass of material covers the slope below, thinning out into a toe which is the farthest point to which the rock mass travelled. Slides may descend very rapidly, and for this reason are usually disastrous in populated areas. Sometimes a forewarning is given by slow creeping and new cracks appearing before the main slip, but it is extremely difficult to predict when the rock face will come down. Many slides occur during periods of intense rainfall, but others have been triggered by earthquakes. In some cases the slope has been made more unstable by rail or road-cuts, or by mine shafts sunk into the rock face.

At midnight on March 22, 1915, the face of a mountain peak above Britannia Mine (on Howe Sound, near Vancouver) broke loose and started an avalanche that ploughed through the mining camp. The mixture of rock, mud, and snow cut a path 300 metres wide down the mountainside, and parts of the camp were buried 15 metres beneath the slide debris when it finally came to rest. Surface cracks had been noticed on the mountain slope, but the area had been judged safe only two days before the disaster in which over sixty people were killed, and 22 injured.

133

During the early hours of January 9, 1965, a major rockslide broke away from the southwest slope of Johnson Peak and blocked the Hope-Princeton Highway in southern British Columbia (Figure 89). At 4:00 a.m., a small earthquake, centred a few kilometres to the north, appears to have triggered a small slide and avalanche which came down the eastern edge of the slide area and stopped traffic on the road. At 7:00 a.m. a second earth tremor was recorded, and a major slide brought down 130 million tons (ten million cubic metres) of rock, mixed with snow, soil, and vegetation. Some of the material descended over one thousand metres to the valley floor, where it overran remnants of an earlier slide and a small lake. As the rock debris mixed with the lake water, some of the valley floor material was driven on in the form of a mudslide. The air blast in front of the slide broke off tree trunks as far as 150 metres up the opposite slope. Four people travelling on the road at the time were buried beneath the debris. It took 21 days to push a path through the slide, and the main highway was eventually diverted over the slide. A potential hazard remains, as the 1965 rockslide left an unstable headwall which, though smaller, represents a future threat.

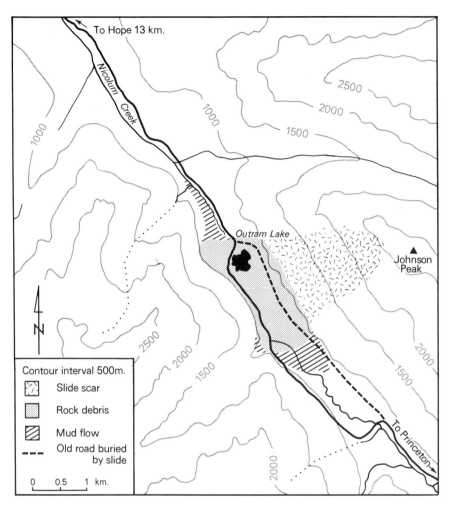

134

Debris flows posed an early threat to rail and road construction in the Canadian Cordillera. Debris flows consist of a mass of water-saturated earth. They slide down hillsides and gullies after heavy rainfall, or during periods of sudden thaw in mountain regions. Material slumps away from a slope, carrying vegetation and boulders buoyed up in the mud.

The Canadian Pacific Railway has faced debris-flow problems since its opening in 1885. An enormous slide on the Thompson River near Ashcroft disrupted the rail-link on a number of occasions when thick beds of silt bordering the river slumped and carried away the rail. The slide was blamed on irrigation of the farmland on the river terraces above the line, and in 1899 the CPR was granted an injunction to prevent the farmers from causing more damage.

An area of frequent debris flows is the Peace River valley, where shales are susceptible to slumping. However, the greatest losses have occurred along the coast of British Columbia, where marine clays are present along many of the fiords. In April 1975, a sub-marine slide created a tidal wave, which caused $500,000 damage in the Kitimat area. Communities on Vancouver Island have also been overwhelmed by debris flows; in December 1973, a tide of mud, rocks, and logs swept into the heart of Port Alice, a pulp mill community at the northern tip of Vancouver Island. The flow came to a halt after 90 seconds, but caused an estimated $500,000 damage. There had been two weeks of heavy rainfall and, just before the slide, ten centimetres of rain fell in 24 hours. Water overflowed the creeks when debris choked the normal runoff. As the debris flow gathered momentum and size, it rolled like a wave into a residential area. Thirty-five homes were evacuated, and one house was knocked 25 metres off its foundations.

Two years later, in November 1975, another debris flow swept down a hillside over several roads and caused extensive flooding in Port Alice. Again, the slide had been caused by heavy rainfall; 12 centimetres had fallen in the previous 14 hours. During the same week, slides occurred elsewhere on Vancouver Island. Many roads were washed out and, in one instance, a debris flow swept over the dam for a local water supply system.

Except on rare occasions, most slope failures occur without warning. By the time the first movement is noticed, it is usually too late to avoid the final slide, and evacuation is necessary. However, if a potential slide area is recognized at an early stage, certain steps can be taken to lessen the damage; drainage holes can be drilled, rock added at the toe, or soil removed from the head of the slope in an attempt to stabilize the slope. Land-use practices such as irrigation farming can be stopped in order to lessen the danger of further sliding. These measures depend on detailed engineering geology studies of the soil and rock.

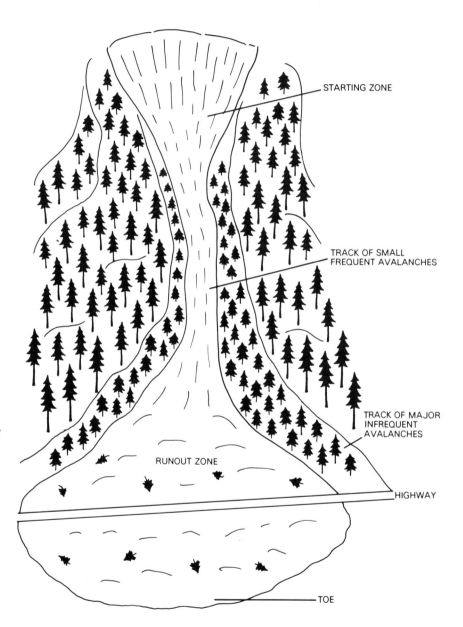

90 A simplified diagram showing the principal features of an avalanche track.

STARTING ZONE

TRACK OF SMALL FREQUENT AVALANCHES

TRACK OF MAJOR INFREQUENT AVALANCHES

RUNOUT ZONE

HIGHWAY

TOE

Avalanches

Avalanches have caused more deaths in British Columbia and the Yukon than any other natural hazard. More than 160 people have been killed by such snow slides, the majority in mining camps. Avalanches are very common in mountain regions, but they only become a hazard when people with little or no experience move into high mountain terrain (Figure 87). Heavier road traffic and tighter rail schedules increase the risk of avalanche damage. Mines and large construction sites in the mountains can be threatened because, with high financial investments, they require continuous operation in winter. The risk of death and injury grows as winter recreation activities, particularly skiing and snowmobiling, increase in remote areas.

One of the worst avalanche disasters occurred in the Chilkoot Pass in 1898, when a continuing blizzard in late March and early April added two metres of wet snow to the pack on the summit of the pass. On April 3, an avalanche swept down from a peak overlooking the trail, and tons of wet snow covered an area of four hectares to a depth of ten metres. Several hundred people were buried, but most were rescued or clawed their way out; 63 bodies were recovered from the snow debris. Despite the large number of people moving through to the Klondike gold fields, this was the only major disaster.

Another major avalanche disaster took place in 1965 at the Granduc mine near Stewart, B.C. Work had begun earlier that year on the development of the copper mine site located in a mountainous region where the annual snowfall exceeds fifteen metres. On February 18, more than 150 men were in camp when a very large avalanche moved down the mountain slope and destroyed half the camp area. Seventy people were buried and of these 43 were rescued. Intensive work has been done at the mine site to protect the area from further disasters during winter operations.

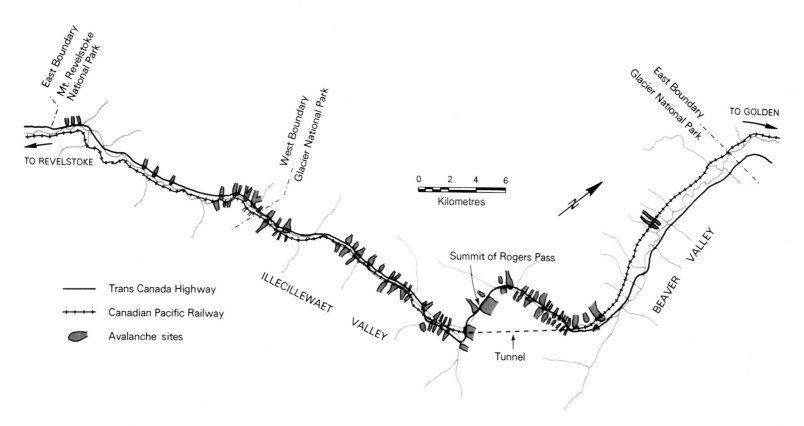

91 Avalanche sites at Roger's Pass, British Columbia. (Simplified from National research Council of Canada, Technical Paper No. 141, 1962)

Avalanche paths are easily recognized on forested slopes because the paths have been stripped of trees. The path consists of the starting zone, where the snow breaks loose and starts to slide; the avalanche track, down which the snow moves; and the runout zone (Figure 90). Avalanche tracks may cross open slopes, but they usually follow rock gullies. The distance that avalanches travel in the runout zone depends on the amount and type of snow. *Dry powder avalanches* can travel considerable distances, and move at speeds up to 70 metres per second (over 250 kilometres an hour). *Wet snow avalanches* travel more slowly (up to 30 metres a second, or 110 kilometres an hour) over shorter distances. The most dangerous type of avalanche is the slab avalanche, which breaks away in large blocks of snow that disintegrate when they get into snow gullies.

Avalanche problems began in the Canadian Cordillera with the opening of the Canadian Pacific Railway at Roger's Pass in 1885 (Figure 91). Many workers lost their lives until the line was finally protected by a total of eight kilometres of snow sheds. Avalanche studies began at the pass in 1954, and an avalanche-safe highway has been maintained successfully since 1962. Records are kept of the frequency, size, and location of snowslides, and winter weather conditions are monitored closely. When snowpack conditions on the slopes overlooking the Trans-Canada Highway are dangerous, traffic is stopped, and potential avalanches are brought down by artillery fire. The explosives are supposed to bring down small avalanches, and thus prevent the snowpack from building up into a large slide which could threaten traffic.

Earthworks, mounds, and dams have been constructed in the runout zones of well-used avalanche paths, in order to slow down a slide that would otherwise overwhelm the road.

Roger's Pass is one of the few transportation routes in the Canadian Cordillera with a history of snowpack monitoring and avalanche control. Ski areas maintain avalanche patrols to monitor snow conditions, post danger signs, or bring down potential slides that threaten ski runs. In changeable weather and snow conditions, skiers can trigger avalanches on the slopes they are traversing, with disastrous results. In 1972, four skiers were killed by an avalanche at Whistler Mountain (north of Vancouver) during a snowstorm.

In most mountainous regions, avalanche slopes which discharge at least once each winter can be recognized as a hazard, because vegetation cannot get established in the runout zone. The problem areas are those affected by the rare, large snowslides, which may occur once in a hundred years. Since vegetation has regrown on the track and runout zone, and any settlement in the area may not be old enough to have experienced a major snowslide, the potential danger can easily escape detection: disaster could strike without warning. Careful studies of snow and slope conditions should always be carried out before mining camps, ski cottage developments or other communities are established in mountainous areas. Sites that are thought to be avalanche-prone should be avoided for permanent settlement.

Floods

The price paid for building on floodplains is high, both in damage and in the cost of flood control programmes. Towns sprang up along river banks, on fertile deltas, and on coastal plains in order to take advantage of the water supply and easy transportation routes. While the communities remained small, the damage was limited, but the flood hazard continues to grow as these towns expand.

Sheet flooding occurs during intense rainstorms in areas where there is inadequate storm drainage. The water, unable to escape into streams or underground, washes over the surface in sheets. This is common on steeply sloping urban land, where the soil surface has been disturbed and covered by asphalt and concrete. Sheet flooding also occurs in open areas where the vegetation and soil are unable to absorb the downpour.

In the Canadian Cordillera, flood waters often rise in late spring, when heavy rainfall combines with snowmelt as temperatures rise in the mountains. Fortunately, river levels tend to rise fairly slowly as the snowpack begins to melt, but sudden warming trends can cause damaging floods. There have been some notable *rainstorm-snowmelt floods* on all the major rivers of British Columbia. Over the last 100 years, the Fraser River has risen to damaging heights more than 25 times, and the inhabitants of the lower Fraser valley began to protect themselves with dykes as early as 1864. In 1894 and 1948, there was serious flooding in the lower Fraser valley as high temperatures released large volumes of meltwater from the mountain snowpacks in the Interior. Although the 1894 flood was the greatest on record, much more detailed information is available on the 1948 damages (Figures 92 and 93). As water levels rose in late May 1948, the river began to erode its banks, and by May 26 there were a series of breaks in the dykes along the Fraser. By June 10, the river had reached its peak: one tenth of all the agricultural land was flooded, 16,000 people were evacuated, and 2,000 homes were damaged. On June 26, the Fraser River at Mission fell below the danger level for the first time in 32 days. The total damage amounted to more than $20 million.

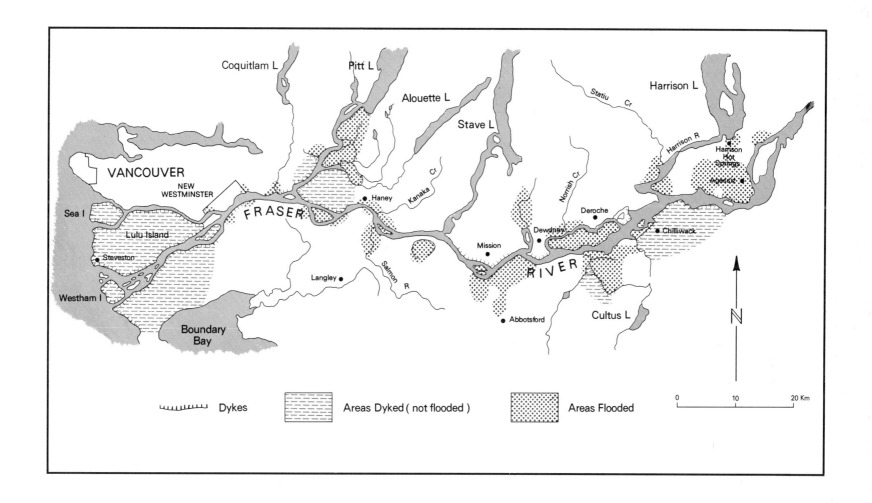

92 A sketch map of the lower Fraser valley showing the location of dykes and land drowned during the 1948 flood.

Dykes   Areas Dyked (not flooded)   Areas Flooded

0   10   20 Km

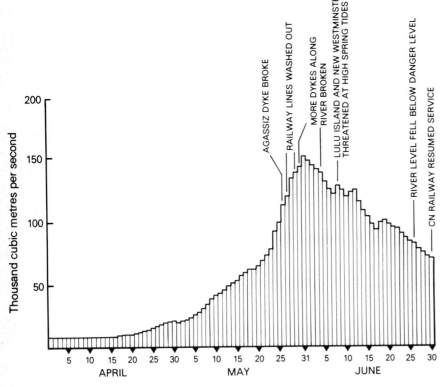

93 The sequence of events during the flooding of the lower Fraser valley in 1948. (Simplified from Fraser River Board, *Preliminary Report on Flood-Control and Hydro-Electric Power in the Fraser River Basin,* 1958)

Ice-jam floods are more common than rainstorm-snowmelt floods in northern British Columbia and the Yukon. During the long winter, ice on the Yukon River and its major tributaries freezes to a depth of almost two metres. If there is a sudden thaw in spring, the river ice may not soften for easy break-up in the usual way. Instead, the rapidly swelling river breaks the ice into large sheets which float downstream, only to be blocked by river narrows, gravel bars and other obstructions. As the sheets grind into each other, the pressure fuses them into a solid mass. Water and ice sheets back up until the ice-jam extends for several kilometres. Water building up behind the jam causes flooding. When the flow becomes powerful enough to break the ice-jam, a flood-wave moves rapidly downstream. Considerable damage can be caused by the volume of water, and by the debris and ice carried along with it.

Coastal flooding is caused by severe storms, unusually high tides or, on rare occasions, by large sea-waves called tsunamis. For example, in 1948, exceptionally high spring tides broke through some of the sea-dykes protecting the Fraser delta and added to the damage caused by the river. A tsunami created in Prince William Sound by the Alaska earthquake in 1964 travelled as far south as California, causing loss of life and damage. At Port Alberni, on the west coast of Vancouver Island, this tsunami inflicted considerable property damage around the harbour.

A number of options are open to floodplain residents. If agricultural and industrial investments on the floodplain are vital to the economy, then engineering works can be built to reduce or control flooding. Dams, dykes, and channel straightening have all been used in British Columbia to reduce the threat of flood damage. Dyking systems were constructed to reclaim and protect floodplain land in the lower Fraser valley, the Pemberton valley, and on Kootenay Flats near the international border. Dams have been built to regulate river flows for both flood control and hydro-electric power generation in the East Kootenay.

It is important to have long records of river flows in order to design engineering works that will withstand the size of floods known to have occurred on a river. The chance of a particular flood flow re-occurring can be predicted if records have been kept for a long time; however, continuous records rarely go back more than fifty years in British Columbia. There is always the risk that a rare super-flood will overwhelm the protective works. Rather than relying totally on dams and dykes, which are not infallible, the use of floodplain land should be restricted. Zoning by-laws, subdivision regulations, and building codes can be used to discourage residential and industrial development, and to encourage agriculture and recreational land uses on floodplains.

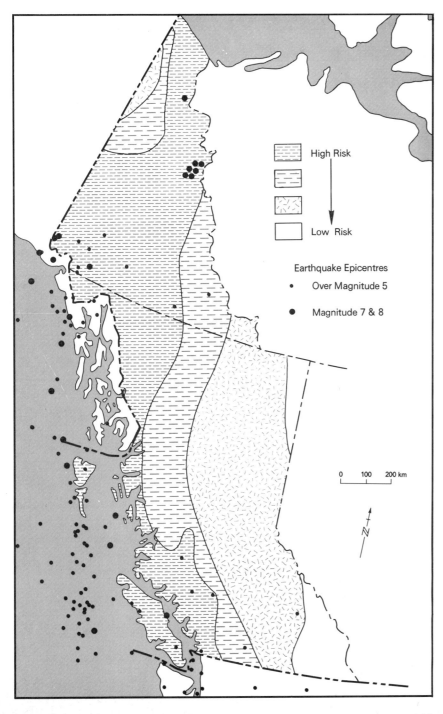

94 The distribution of seismic risk and the location of known earthquake epicentres in the Canadian Cordillera and adjacent region.

High Risk

Low Risk

Earthquake Epicentres

• Over Magnitude 5

● Magnitude 7 & 8

0   100   200 km

Earthquakes

Damage from earthquakes has been extremely low, in comparison with other areas such as California and Alaska. However, western Canada has experienced large earthquakes, and one could cause considerable damage in the future. During the last century, the number of reported earthquakes increased rapidly as the population grew. However, even today, the picture would be distorted, if it were not for a network of seismographic stations which record earthquakes in the large, uninhabited regions of British Columbia and the Yukon.

There are fewer earthquakes in the Interior of British Columbia and the Yukon than in California. The main belt of seismic activity lies along a zone of faults off the outer coast between the Queen Charlotte Islands and Vancouver Island (Figure 94). The greatest earthquake risk is concentrated along the insular belt and the mainland coast.

Seismographs measure ground motion experienced during an earthquake. From these records, the magnitude of an earthquake can be calculated on the Richter scale. Tremors over magnitude 2 can be felt by people, but sensitive seismographs can detect much smaller disturbances. Earthquakes over magnitude 5 can cause property damage, while tremors of magnitude 7 or more can inflict major losses in inhabited areas. Figure 95 describes some of the larger earthquakes experienced in western Canada, in comparison with other well known earthquakes.

An earthquake registering 8.1 on the Richter scale was experienced in the Queen Charlotte Islands in August 1949, but there was only minor damage in the sparsely-populated area. The most damaging earthquake in British Columbia occurred in June 23, 1946, in the Strait of Georgia between Powell River and Courtenay. There were landslides and property damage on Vancouver Island as a result of this magnitude 7.3 tremor.

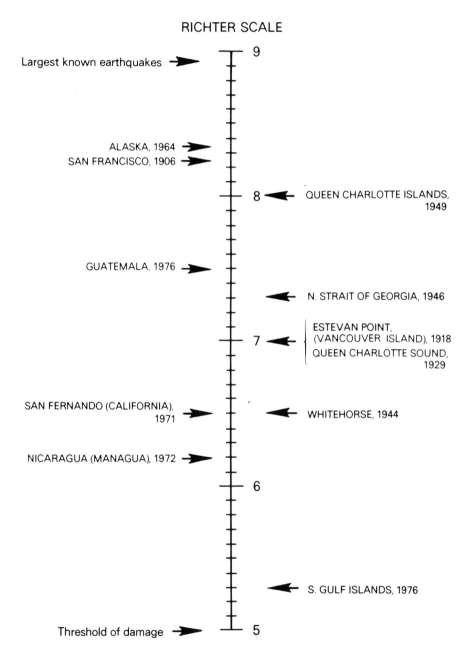

The extent of earthquake damage depends on the ground motion, geology, soils, and building construction. There is less ground motion away from the epicentre (the place on the earth's surface immediately above the origin of the earthquake). If the epicentre is located in a populated area, the damage can be enormous. Loose soils can liquefy during an earthquake, resulting in flow slides and building collapse. The alluvial sands and silts of the Fraser delta are a potential hazard because of the risk of liquefaction.

The potential damage increases with urban development. Unfortunately, many people are unaware of the risk, or do not take the risk seriously. People should neither exaggerate the potential hazard nor be complacent about a damaging earthquake in a populated area. In the early hours of May 16, 1976, a magnitude 5.3 tremor, centred in the Gulf Islands, woke Vancouver residents less than 25 kilometres away. A stronger earthquake close to a population centre could result in major losses. The National Building Code adopted by municipalities requires that buildings should be constructed to withstand certain levels of ground motion. While many buildings were in existence before these regulations were introduced, in the future it will be important to design structures that can withstand potential earthquakes.

Forest Fires

Fire scars on old trees, charcoal found in soil profiles, and the reports of early explorers give ample evidence of large-scale lightning fires in the past. However, there was a dramatic increase in forest fires when settlers, prospectors, loggers and railway builders moved into western Canada. For example, in 1908, Fernie was destroyed by a fire which took 25 lives and caused property damage valued at $5 million.

The greatest risk of forest fire occurs during the dry summer months. Many fires are caused by lightning, but land clearing, logging operations, and railroads have been important sources of man-made fires; recreationists are also major offenders. Forest fire statistics are not easy to compile and are not always reliable, because many fires in remote areas were never seen by forest rangers. However, as early as 1915, travellers' and campers' fires were blamed for 30 per cent of the total number of forest fires recorded.

Fires continue to occur, but modern controls have reduced their extent. Organized forest fire protection can be traced back to the turn of the century. By the 1920s, aircraft were being used for fire detection and transportation. Their effectiveness increased dramatically after World War II, and forest fire-fighting now depends heavily on water-bombing. Certain types of fire are still very difficult to control; there is no effective method of coping with a large crown fire that spreads through the tops of coniferous trees during high winds.

Fires are not always harmful. Slash burning is commonly used to reduce the hazards from logging debris and to prepare suitable ground conditions for planting young trees in newly logged areas. Controlled fires can also be used to improve wildlife habitat, and to control insects and diseases. Following a fire, all the requirements for good germination and early seedling growth are usually present. The mineral soil is exposed, more sunlight reaches ground level, and there is no competing vegetation.

Few fires are intense enough to cause long-lasting soil damage, but there are other effects on the forest environment. Many small animals may be killed, although the new growth provides habitat for large species such as deer and moose, which prefer young, succulent vegetation. The destruction of vegetation can have a major impact on local water resources; more water runs off as there is little vegetation to trap the moisture, and the increased runoff can erode the soil and wash it into nearby streams.

A forest fire is only a hazard to the extent that it threatens life and property or destroys mature timber that was to have been logged in the near future. In fact, many valuable forests owe their existence to fire. Some tree species have adapted to fire disturbance and some depend on fire for their reproduction. For example, jack pine (*Pinus banksiana*), lodgepole pine (*Pinus contorta*), and black spruce (*Picea mariana*) establish themselves after a fire. These conifers have closed cones which stay on the trees for many years; the cone scales are held together by a resinous substance that melts at about 50 degrees C. The thick scales protect the seeds during a fire, while the heat opens the cones to disperse their seeds. The policy of forest fire protection and control disturbs this process and some valuable coniferous stands will not be renewed. The fire hazard must be controlled near populated areas, but forest fires are natural in uninhabited regions.

Forest Pests and Diseases

Infestations of defoliating insects and bark beetles are a serious problem in British Columbia. Their impact is less severe in the Yukon, where they tend to attack hardwood species which have no commercial importance at present. Infectious diseases caused by fungi and bacteria can inflict major damage, but losses from them in western Canada have been generally minor. Quite serious local damage can be caused by unfavourable climatic conditions, soil nutrient losses, and air pollution.

The major losses are caused by *insects*, which often attack trees already weakened by other agents. A wide range of damaging insects invades the bark or foliage of valuable coniferous species (Table 6). The attacks usually lead to the discolouration and the death of the foliage. If severe, the infestations will kill young trees and retard the growth of or kill mature stands. Different insects infest different species of trees, and some native conifers have developed resistance to their attacks. However, the danger in recent years has been the importation of new insect pests with exotic seedlings brought in for replanting programmes. These insects could well adopt native coniferous species as their new hosts, and the trees would have little resistance to such attacks.

Insect infestations can be handled in a number of ways. Slash burning on logged sites helps to remove attractive havens for insects. Pest populations can be controlled by applying insecticides and by logging or burning infested stands. Natural predators of the insects have been encouraged, although they have not always been successful. Scientists are now trying to breed strains of otherwise harmless insects which will attack the pests. In the future, the careful monitoring of imports and the use of more resistant tree species will help to reduce the hazard. Once a coniferous stand is seriously infested, the only solution is to harvest the trees.

Source: Canadian Forestry Service,
1967.

Table 6:
Forest Insect Pests Common to British Columbia and The Yukon

Insect	Trees Attacked	Damage	Outbreaks
Spruce budworm	Engelmann spruce, white spruce, alpine fir, Douglas fir	Loss of foliage. Trees killed after 5 years of successive defoliations.	First reported in 1909. Persistent in some areas during recent years.
Mountain pine beetle	Western white pine, ponderosa pine, lodgepole pine	Bores into trunk leaving "pitch tubes" of resin and boring dust on the bark. Loss of foliage.	Extensive outbreaks in Sub-alpine and Montane forests.
Douglas-fir beetle	Most destructive enemy of mature Douglas fir	Attacks bark. Foliage fades and dies.	Outbreaks on coast short-lived, but can last many years in Interior.
Douglas-fir tussock moth	Douglas fir, especially in the dry Interior. Occasionally attacks Engelmann spruce.	Defoliation	First reported in Interior B.C. in 1916. Periodic, severe, but not extensive infestations.
Black-headed budworm	Hemlock and tree firs. Douglas fir and Sitka spruce may also be attacked.	Defoliation and top-killing.	Fairly frequent outbreaks lasting 2-3 years. Vancouver Island and Queen Charlotte Islands.
Western hemlock looper	Western hemlock. Also attacks Sitka spruce and amabilis fir on coast, and grand fir and alpine fir in Interior.	Attacks newly-opened buds. Trees killed in first year.	Periodic outbreaks in coastal forests Generally last 3 years.

Animals seldom become pests, but they can cause damage by grazing on young shoots and thus inhibiting the growth of trees. On rare occasions, deer and elk can create an overgrazing problem on their winter range when herds are confined to small areas because of heavy snowfall.

Plant pests are the weeds or unwanted species which compete with the young seedlings planted in reforested areas. Deciduous species such as maple, alder, and birch are often the first to invade a cleared site and compete with the more valued coniferous trees for sunlight, moisture, and soil nutrients. Herbicides and slash burning are used to prepare the site and reduce the competition from weed species.

Infectious diseases are caused by fungi and bacteria that attack trees to obtain essential food materials. They often invade mature stands which are already weakened by other factors and cause stem diseases, needleblights, and needle and cone rusts. Coniferous trees are attacked by a number of stem and foliage rusts which are capable of killing seedlings and retarding the growth of mature trees. The losses from tree rusts have been fairly small in British Columbia and the Yukon, but new diseases such as white pine blister rust have been introduced by imported trees.

Non-infectious diseases develop because of unfavourable changes in the climate, air pollution, or soil nutrient losses. Trees vary in their susceptibility to damage, depending on the species and on the age and vigour of the stand. Late winter frosts can cause local damage. Although very low temperatures are needed to kill trees, temperatures just below freezing can damage young foliage which has not hardened off. Tree crowns can be broken off by heavy accumulations of snow, and violent windstorms can produce patches of blowdown. In mountain regions, *winterkill* occurs when coniferous foliage is exposed to warm, dry winds when the ground is frozen. The trees are unable to replace the water lost by transpiration, and the needles dry out, turn red, and die. These red-belts can be traced along the mountain slopes, following the pathway of the drying winds. The damaged trees are weakened and susceptible to attack by bacteria, fungi, and other pests.

Air pollution can inflict severe damage on natural vegetation. Fumes from heavy metal smelters destroy the surrounding vegetation, if the sulphur dioxide emissions are concentrated. The forest area in the Columbia Valley had already declined in the early 1900s because of logging, fire, and disease. However, increased production from the Trail smelter completed the destruction. Sulphur dioxide emissions from the heavy metal smelter reached a peak in the late 1920s, when as much as ten tons of sulphur were released into the atmosphere each month. The area affected by the fumes extended 23 kilometres upwind and 95 kilometres downwind from the smelter. To the north, fume-damaged areas supported a limited growth of aspen and willow. Very little vegetation was left between Trail and the international border, and soil erosion was severe. The conifers were particularly sensitive to injury; their needles were exposed for a long time, as they stayed on the trees for several years. Air pollution controls were improved during the 1940s, and within ten years the vegetation had re-established itself in the Columbia Valley around Trail.

Further Reading

General

Much has been written about the natural resources of British Columbia but the material tends to be widely scattered and difficult to find. Sources on the Yukon Territory are more limited. Few overviews are available and most of the information is to be found in specialized government reports.

The most useful sources of statistical information on natural resources are the *Canada Year Book* (published annually since 1905) and the census reports of Statistics Canada. The published proceedings of the British Columbia Natural Resources Conference held each year from 1948 to 1967 provide another source of statistics as well as insights into the viewpoints of government, industry and university representatives.

The *British Columbia Atlas of Resources* edited by J.D. Chapman and B.D. Turner, was a special publication prepared for the Conference held in 1956. Although much of the material on resource development becomes quickly outdated, the atlas provides a benchmark for comparison with more recent times. The most outstanding contribution to the discussion of B.C.'s natural resources during this period was *The Living Land* written by Roderick Haig-Brown and published by William Morrow & Co. (New York) in 1961. This book is to be valued for its insights into the availability of natural resources and management problems associated with their use. More statistical information was included in the 1964 Conference publication, *Inventory of the Natural Resources of British Columbia*.

A more recent publication examines distinct facets of B.C.'s resources and the provincial economy. This is *British Columbia*, a book edited by J. Lewis Robinson and published in 1972 by the University of Toronto Press. The volume is part of a regional series produced for the International Geographical Congress held in Canada in 1972.

Two government publications are useful for observing short-term trends in resource use. These are *British Columbia, Manual of Resources and Development* and *British Columbia, Summary of Economic Activity*. Both are produced annually by the B.C. Department of Industrial Development, Trade and Commerce. A large number of more specialized government reports are released each year; the bibliography included within each issue of the journal *B.C. Studies* is a good starting point for tracing them.

The literature on the Yukon Territory is not as voluminous. One source of information is a report produced by D.W. Carr & Associates in 1968, *The Yukon Economy, Its Potential for Growth and Development*. The Final Report and numerous Background Studies provide overviews of resource potential and recent developments. Anyone interested in tracing more specialized publications should refer to the *Yukon Bibliography Update 1963-1970* by C.A. Hemstock and G.A. Cook. This volume was produced in 1973 by the Boreal Institute for Northern Studies, University of Alberta, Edmonton.

The most recent and worthwhile addition to the literature on resource exploration and development in northern British Columbia and the Yukon is a book written by K.J. Rea, *The Political Economy of Northern Development* (Science Council of Canada, Background Study No. 36, 1976). This report documents the social and economic implications of projects ranging from new mines to extension of the existing transportation network in the north. The reader learns about northern British Columbia and the Yukon within the context of northern Canada as a whole.

Minerals, Energy and Water

Information on metal-mining, coal and petroleum resources is widely scattered but fortunately western Canada has been blessed with a policy of excellence in government publications since the early days of mining. The two principal sources are publications of the B.C. Department of Mines and Petroleum Resources and the Geological Survey of Canada.

Since 1874, the B.C. Department of Mines and Petroleum Resources has published its *Annual Reports* (statistics, descriptions of exploration and mining activity throughout the province), *Bulletins* (thorough descriptions of individual mining camps), and *Hydro-Carbon By-Product Reserves* (quantitative information on all oil and natural gas fields in the province). The report of the Provincial Coal Task Force, *Coal in British Columbia, A Technical Appraisal* (February 1976) documents resource potential and development of this fossil fuel.

The Geological Survey of Canada provides most of the *geological maps* of British Columbia and has published many descriptions of mining camps in the Yukon Territory and B.C. in its *Annual* and *Summary Reports* (e.g. the early exploratory travels of G.M. Dawson, A. Selwyn, R.G. McConnell, J. Richardson), and *Memoirs, Bulletins* and *Papers* (monographs on regional geology and mining camps).

Other important technical descriptions of mines have been published in the *Canadian Institute of Mining and Metallurgy Bulletin*, the *Canadian Mining Journal* and the *Western Miner*.

Three excellent overviews are "Economic Minerals of Western Canada" in *Geology and Economic Minerals of Canada* (Geological Survey of Canada, 1970), "Tectonic History and Mineral Deposits of the Western Cordillera" (Canadian Institute of Mining and Metallurgy, Special Volume No. 8, 1966) and "Metallogeny of the Canadian Cordillera" (Canadian Institute of Mining and Metallurgy, Transactions, Volume 74, 1971).

A number of recent federal and provincial government reports document the sources and growing demand for electric power. The B.C. Energy Board published a ten-volume *Provincial Power Study* in 1972. The B.C. Hydro and Power Authority reviewed the supply and demand for electric power in their report, *Alternatives 1975-1990*, released in 1976. The federal government published a two-volume report on the *Hydro-Electric Resources Survey of the Central Yukon Territory* (Department of Indian Affairs and Northern Development, 1968). Background Study Volume 6 of the Carr Report documents the power resources of the Yukon Territory (see above).

The best sources of information on water resources are the publications of Environment Canada, the Geological Survey of Canada and the B.C. Water Resources Service. An overview of the quantity, quality, and use of water resources is presented in the *Canada Water Year Book 1975* (Environment Canada). Another report produced by Environment Canada is *Magnitude of Floods in British Columbia* (Water Survey of Canada, 1972). This provides quantitative information on stream flows within the province. The Geological Survey of Canada has published a report on *Groundwater in Canada* (Economic Geology Report No. 24, 1968) which provides a description of the groundwater resources of the Cordillera.

Other good sources of information on specific river basins include the *Final Report* and twelve *Technical Supplements* produced in 1973-4 under the Canada-British Columbia Okanagan Basin Agreement. Details of the 1948 Fraser flood are provided in the *Preliminary* and *Final Report on Flood-Control and Hydro-Electric Power in the Fraser River Basin* produced by the B.C. Fraser River Board in 1958 and 1963 respectively. The links between freshwater resources and oceanic waters are explored in a report by M.L. Barker, *Water Resources and Related Land Uses, Strait of Georgia-Puget Sound Basin* (Environment Canada, Geographical Paper No. 56, 1974). The report is accompanied by two large wall-maps showing the distribution and use of water resources in this region.

Land and Forest Resources

The best introduction to the climate of western Canada is provided by a book written by W.G. Kendrew and D. Kerr, *The Climate of British Columbia and the Yukon Territory* (Ottawa Queen's Printer, 1955). More quantitative information is given in monthly and annual statistical reports published by Environment Canada, (e.g. Temperature and Precipitation Tables, monthly).

Soil maps and accompanying reports are published by Canada, Department of Agriculture and by the B.C. Department of the Environment. Another helpful publication is *Permafrost in Canada, Its Influence on Northern Development* by R.J.E. Brown (University of Toronto Press, 1970).

The Canadian Forestry Service has produced two excellent guides to natural vegetation. These are the *Forest*

Regions of Canada by T.S. Rowe (published in 1972) and *Native Trees of Canada* by R.S. Hosie (published in 1969). Perhaps the best known guide is a book by C.P. Lyons, *Trees, Shrubs and Flowers to Know in British Columbia* (Vancouver: J.M. Dent & Sons). V.J. Krajina provides a more technical description of plant communities in his two edited volumes entitled *Ecology of Western North America* (Department of Botany, University of British Columbia, 1965).

Since 1945, the B.C. Forest Service has produced *Annual Reports* and published material on particular topics. These include introductions to *Management of British Columbia's Forest Lands* (Publication B 57, 1973), *Sustained Yield from British Columbia's Forest Lands* (Publication B 55, 1973) and *The Principal Commercial Trees of British Columbia*. In 1972, this agency published a report on *The Sawmilling Industry of British Columbia*. The B.C. Department of Industrial Development, Trade and Commerce produced a *B.C. Pulp and Paper Industry* report in 1971.

There are a number of key references for anyone interested in the history of the forest industry and logging practices in B.C. These include H.N. Whitford and R.D. Craig, *Forests of British Columbia* (Commission of Conservation, Ottawa, 1918) and the reports of several *Royal Commissions on Forest Resources*. The most notable are the reports of the Sloan Commission (1945 and 1956) and the Pearse Commission (published in November, 1976).

The best summary of the growth of the provincial forest industry is provided by A. Farley in his chapter "The Forest Resource" in *British Columbia* (edited by J. Lewis Robinson). An illustrated description is given by E. Gould in *Logging: British Columbia's Logging History* (Saanichton: Hancock House). G.W. Taylor's *Timber* (Vancouver: J.J. Douglas, 1975) offers a history of the provincial forest industry.

The status of the Yukon's logging industry and forest potential is reviewed in the Carr Report, Background Study No. 8, *Forest Resource Study* (see Further Reading — Introduction).

The literature on agriculture is much more limited. A useful source of information is the B.C. Department of Agriculture *Annual Report*. M.A. Ormsby reviews the early history in her article, "Agricultural development in British Columbia," (*Agricultural History*, Volume 19, 1945, pp. 11-20). The most valuable sources are regional descriptions such as T. Weir, *Ranching in the Southern Interior Plateau of British Columbia* (Ottawa, 1964), L. Nelson, "Range resources in the Interior of British Columbia," (*B.C. Perspectives*, Volume 1, 1972, pp. 19-39) and B.C. Department of Agriculture, *Agriculture in the Central Kootenay Region* (Creston, 1970). A brochure, *Keeping the Options Open* (Victoria, 1974) documents the aims of the B.C. Land Commission.

Agriculture in the Yukon Territory is discussed in the Carr Report, Background Study No. 4.

The federal government is co-operating with the provinces under the Canada Land Inventory programme to produce a series of *Land Capability Maps* for every area of Canada. The map topics appropriate to this chapter are *Land Capability for Forestry, Land Capability for Agriculture* and *Present Land Use*. Information concerning the distribution of the most suitable land for various uses is combined on a series of regional *Land Capability Analysis* maps. To date, these regional overview maps have been produced for the Cariboo and Peace River districts. An index map of Canada indicates the availability of completed maps of each series for every area in the country.

Fish and Wildlife

Two excellent publications describe the mammal populations of western Canada. These are *The Mammals of Canada* by A.W.F. Banfield, published for the National Museum of Natural Sciences and the National Museums of Canada by the University of Toronto Press (1974) and *The Mammals of British Columbia* by I. McTaggart-Cowan and C.J. Guiguet (B.C. Provincial Museum, 6th printing, 1965). Both books are superbly illustrated with drawings, photographs and maps showing the distribution of each species. D. Blood has produced an attractive, less technical volume, *Rocky Mountain Wildlife* (Saanichton: Hancock House, 1976) which contains many colour photographs. V. Geist's book, *Mountain Sheep and Man in the Northern Wilds* (Ithaca: Cornell University Press, 1975) is a well written account of the author's research on wildlife in north-central B.C.

Several map series document the distribution of critical wildlife habitats in British Columbia and the Yukon Territory. Canada Land Inventory maps show *Land Capability for Waterfowl* and *Land Capability for Ungulates*. The *Land Use Information Series* produced by Environment Canada show the distribution of wildlife habitats, wildlife reserves and areas covered by trap-lines in the Yukon Territory.

A number of government reports address hunting and trapping in western Canada. The *Annual Reports* of the B.C. Fish and Wildlife Branch contain information on wildlife management practices. Economic studies published by the Fish and Wildlife Branch include *The Value of Resident Hunting in British Columbia* (Study Report No. 6, 1972). Another publication to look for is *The Canadian Fur Industry* produced by Canada, Department of Agriculture in 1971. The Carr Report, Background Study Volume 4 discusses hunting, trapping and fishing in the Yukon Territory.

Commercial fishing has received considerable attention in British Columbia. The federal Fisheries and Marine Service (Environment Canada) publishes *Annual Reports, Catch Statistics* and special studies. Examples of the special reports include *The Development of the Fraser River Canning Industry, 1885-1913* by D.J. Reid (1973) and *Some Economic Aspects of Commercial Fishing in B.C.* published in 1973.

The *Annual Reports* of the International Pacific Salmon Fisheries Commission are useful sources of information. The most detailed study of the history of salmon fishing in British Columbia is *Salmon: Our Heritage* by C.P. Lyons (Vancouver, Mitchell Press, 1969). *Fishing: British Columbia's Commercial Fishing Industry* by J.E. Forester and A.D. Forester (Saanichton: Hancock House, 1975) takes a broader look at the history of the industry. The book is particularly well illustrated with old photographs.

A number of publications focus on sport fishing. Two reports of the B.C. Fish and Wildlife Branch are of interest: *The Value of Freshwater Sport Fishing in British Columbia* and *The Value of Non-Resident Sport Fishing in British Columbia*. (Victoria, 1970). The federal Fisheries and Marine Service published *British Columbia Sport Fishermen* by W.F. Sinclair in 1972.

The most recent reports on northern fishing include *Yukon Fishery Resource: Its Existing Role and Its Future Potential* and *The Economic Value of the Yukon Sport Fishery*, both published by the Fisheries and Marine Service in 1973.

Parks and Recreation

Specialized reports on particular aspects of recreation are available. These include *The B.C. Ski Industry and Its Economic Effects*, a publication prepared for the B.C. Department of Travel Industry in 1974 and *Resident Boating in Georgia Strait* by G. Mos and M. Hamilton (Fisheries and Marine Service, Technical Report No. PAC 11-74-5).

Information on the national parks of western Canada can be found in a number of books, articles and guides. A helpful overview of the philosophy behind planning national parks is contained in J.G. Nelson's book, *Canada's National Parks: Past, Present and Future* (Montreal: Harvest House, 1970). Particular parks are described in *Pacific Rim: An Ecological Approach to a New Canadian National Park*, by J.G. Nelson and L.D. Cordes (Studies in Land Use History, Landscape Change, No. 4, University of Calgary, 1972), R.A. Beatty's article, "Pacific rim National Park," *Canadian Geographical Journal*, Volume 92, 1976 and an article by J.B. Theberge, "Kluane: a national park two-thirds under ice," *Canadian Geographical Journal*, Volume 91, 1975.

There is more material about British Columbia's provincial parks. The *Annual Reports* of the B.C. Parks Branch provide useful information on short-term changes in the park system. A *B.C. Parks List* is updated annually. In 1975, the Planning Division of the Parks Branch published a book of maps entitled *British Columbia's Park System: a Graphic Presentation* (Planning Report No. 1) which shows the changing distribution of parks, campgrounds, and park visitors in recent years. D. Tatreau and B. Tatreau offer more general descriptions in their book, *The Parks of British Columbia, A Comprehensive Guide to B.C.'s Provincial and National Parks* (Vancouver: Mitchell Press, 1976).

The Canada Land Inventory has published a series of maps showing *Land Capability for Recreation*. The B.C. government has produced maps for many of the larger provincial parks, including Tweedsmuir, Strathcona and Garibaldi. Spectacular topographic maps of some of the older national parks have been produced by the federal government.

Natural Hazards

There are no general descriptions of landslide hazard in the Canadian Cordillera. However, two articles are of special interest: W.H. Mathews and K.C. McTaggart, "The Hope landslide, British Columbia," *Proceedings of the Geological Association of Canada*, Volume 20 (1969), pp. 65-75; and G.H. Eisbacher, "Natural slope failure, northeastern Skeena Mountains," *Canadian Geotechnical Journal*, Volume 8 (1971), pp. 384-390.

Avalanche hazard and control measures at Roger's Pass, B.C. are discussed in an article by P.A. Schaerer: "Planning avalanche defense works for the Trans-Canada Highway at Roger's Pass, B.C., *Engineering Journal*, Volume 45 (1962), pp. 31-38.

A number of publications referring to floods in western Canada are listed in the section on water. Additional material is found in W.R.D. Sewell's book, *Water Management and Floods in the Fraser River Basin* (University of Chicago Department of Geography Research Paper No. 100, 1965).

The following articles are the best sources of information on earthquakes: W.G. Milne and A.G. Davenport, "Distribution of earthquake risk in Canada, *Bulletin of the Seismological Society of America*, Volume 59 (1969), pp. 729-754. K. Whitham, W.G. Milne and W.E.T. Smith, "The new seismic zoning map for Canada, 1970 edition,"

Canadian Underwriter, June 1970, and K. Whitham, "The estimation of seismic risk in Canada," *Geoscience Canada*, Volume 2 (1975), pp. 133-140.

Very little has been written specifically about forest fires in British Columbia and the Yukon Territory. Estimates of the number, size and probable cost of damage are published in the *Annual Reports* of the B.C. Forest Service.

Two excellent introductions to forest pests and disease are *Important Forest Insects and Diseases of Natural Concern to Canada, the United States and Mexico* (Canadian Forestry Service, 1967) and *Common Tree Diseases of British Columbia* (Canadian Forestry Service 1969). The Canadian Forestry Service also publishes *Forest Insect and Disease Surveys* each year. Agricultural pests and diseases are important in British Columbia but were not discussed in the text because all the available published material is highly specialized.

Metric Conversion

Length
1 centimetre = 10 millimetres = 0.39 inches
1 metre = 100 centimetres = 3.28 feet
1 kilometre = 1,000 metres = 0.62 miles

Area
1 hectare = 10,000 square metres = 2.47 acres
1 square kilometre = 100 hectares = 247 acres = 0.386 square miles

Volume
1 litre = 0.22 gallons (imperial)
1 cubic metre = 35.315 cubic feet
Measures of wood volume: 1 cubic metre = 0.353 cunits = 5.886 board feet (Coast lumber) = 6.139 board feet (Interior lumber)

Weight
1 kilogram = 1,000 grams = 2.205 pounds
1 ton (metric) = 1,000 kilograms = 1.016 long tons = 0.907 short tons

INDEX